Mission Afoot

Volume 1

Mission Afoot

Volume 1

A journey of discovery about life itself inspired by
the 200 mile Coast to Coast walk across Britain

SIMON BRANSON

authorHOUSE®

AuthorHouse™
1663 Liberty Drive
Bloomington, IN 47403
www.authorhouse.com
Phone: 1-800-839-8640

Published by AuthorHouse   02/29/2012

ISBN: 978-1-4678-8981-0 (sc)
ISBN: 978-1-4678-8982-7 (e)

Synopsis

The author uses our fundamental human capability of walking, to most of us an everyday subconscious activity, and turns it into a thought provoking journey exploring the journey of life itself inspired by the experiences on Wainwright's famous 200 mile Coast to Coast route and punctuated, to add emotion, with musical references.

In today's world why do we still bother to walk when we don't have to? What experiences could it possibly bring that outweigh being extremely cold, completely wet through, at times absolutely knackered, and so intoxicating that you would do it day after day after day?

Do not be fooled; this journey is a challenging one, some of you will be able to accomplish it, some of you will begin to understand it, but only a few will really connect with it. If reading was analogous to listening to your Radio you need to start by tuning into the right wavelength to have a chance of getting there. I hope you can discover how to set yourself free.

"I saw the angel in the marble and carved until I set him free" Michelangelo.

You have the potential to be set free . . . .

About the Author

Simon L Branson was born in Chesterfield in 1959 the only son of Gerald and Mary Branson. His parents were married in 1951 after his father left the Navy and started work in the post office. They took the job opportunities so moved to Yorkshire then again to Chester when Simon was aged 9 and remained until he left school.

In the house in Chester was a piano and Simon began piano lessons, a piano has been a major consideration ever since when it comes to moving house. Simons desire to see how a thing worked was shown at an early age. When he was about ten his uncle gave him a wall clock which no longer worked so he took it apart, seeing dozens of cogs all over the floor his father went for the dust pan and brush, but it's still in working order 40 years on.

After spotting a veteran car, a 1936 Morris, in a field his father bought it and three years later, now aged seventeen, Simon had fully restored it, the press got to know which led to an interview on the local radio station motoring show.

He would spend every summer term with a family in France which influenced his taste for good food and fine wine. As well as the piano Simon also started to dabble in Art and produced some oil paintings, also working in an Antique shop on Saturdays.

Led by his desire to understand how things worked, he chose to study Physics at Liverpool, indulging of course in walking and rock climbing. After graduation he went on to study Electronics at Hatfield. His first job was at Marconi, becoming a senior electronics design engineer after 5 years, which served as a launching pad to a career spanning 25 years with many prestigious companies, becoming a Chartered Engineer, Chartered Physicist and a member of the Institute of Physics along the way whilst maintaining his love of art, classical music and the piano, washed down with some real ale.

He now enjoys living and working near the Peak District National Park which affords plenty of good walking. His son, Simon G, is studying law, having also gone to Liverpool, and his wife, Deborah, is the district nurse.

Preface

There comes a time in life when you can reach an overwhelming urge to express your thoughts, your emotions, and you have to do just whatever it takes to get something out of your system. A mechanism has to be found for each of us, hopefully positive but sometimes in a negative way, to release the energy. In this case I would like to start with a big thank you for the guy who invented writing.

The need to express something can reach a point where it's not even possible to move on until you've have a full download and got it completely out of your system. For me, in me, it frequently builds up to a point where my brain becomes overloaded and if I don't decant the information I become irritable, can't sleep, and generally become an annoying pain to those around me, ask my wife.

In my line of work I deal with problem solving all the time, I remain unsettled until I have a solution, a self induced pressure is on and I remain focused until the problem is resolved and the pressure can be released. I've also come to realise, after many years of contemplation, that it's the way my brain is wired and consequently what I do for a living unavoidably spills over into my day to day life, although acceptance of this fact took a little longer.

I'd like to believe the way I'm wired serves to move me forward as a human being, ensures continued learning and ultimately brings rewards in various unforeseen guises. Although it can be very frustrating at times, certainly more often than I'd choose it to be, I can usually look back and find comfort in the learning experience, or achievement, may it be a new discovery, a unique creative idea, a new design or an invention.

A foray into authorship has been a goal of mine for many years; the problem has not been so much the beginning but how to end! Yes, it's having an ending that's been the main obstacle I've been struggling with. Life starts but where does it end, and how can you write about it until it's happened? What would be the objective of an open ended book? Further, I've been reconciled to the fact that if there is no ending then starting is pointless and until I start I have no problem. So, if I had an ending I would have some boundaries to work within, that which was preventing me beginning is gone, problem solved.

There are many books about walking, some describe the route in great detail, some include exquisite photos of the landscape and indicate paths to guide the walker, and some describe the difficulty of each section and how much you're likely to sweat. A Composer uses the sound from instruments to bring us music, an Artist may use a canvas and an Author words, but essentially they are all attempting to convey an emotion, an event, an opinion, a mood . . . .

As creative people, a facet of human nature inherent in all of us to some degree, we use our chosen medium to convey our message. The observer of the finished work will hopefully understand, or "get", the message, and sadly some will not.

I'm not going to describe the route in detail, that's already been done many times, or portray how much physical effort and sweat is required climbing these hills. This is my canvas to express an understanding of why people bother to walk at all. For that I need to go on a journey and attempt to unravel something about the journey of life itself.

A note of great importance; I wouldn't have been able to do this without my wife. Thanks Deborah.

Chapter 0

Eureka! At last, I have an ending, a conclusion, something that is finite, and consequently, working backwards of course, I also have a beginning. You'll have to stick with it to discover the rest, I know things may appear somewhat loosely defined at the moment but at least I have an envelope to work within and as events unfold I'm confident the conclusion will be able to take care of itself. I always say "once the problem is understood a solution is not far away".

What's the end then? I knew you were going to ask that question! If you're asking how, after all this time, I found an ending the answer is I used the end of a physical journey as the analogy. As with most solutions this sounds quite simple now.

Where are we going? We're going to travel across Britain, or to be more precise, from St Bees Head in Cumbria to Robin Hoods Bay in North Yorkshire, on foot.

Why? Good, that's the question you should ask and my desire to impart, and so that the answer is satisfactory, I'm going to let you answer that one yourself.

Have you ever been for a walk? No not to the shops, a walk? We've got two dogs and I thought I'd been for a walk, I thought they had too. When I was younger my dad sometimes took me for a walk. When I was very young, I mean very young, he was a postman so he must have been for many a walk.

We used to go into the Derbyshire dales, I remember doing this before the age of 10, mum would stay in the car, her legs didn't work very well, and we'd go for a walk. Monsal Dale was a favourite. For how long and how far, at that age, didn't register. We just went for a walk. Sometimes we would go with other cousins from mums family, Lathkill Dale, Clumber Park, Froggatt Edge . . . .

Did we have the right equipment? You're joking, I never even know there was any equipment—people just walked. The Weather? I never gave it a thought, if it rained we got wet. Once, when we were out in the Derbyshire Dales, Calver to be precise, we met someone my mum and dad knew. He was walking on his own and, just for a while, stopped to talk. Then I noticed for the first time someone with a rucksack on their back and wearing muddy boots. Mum and dad told me he liked walking, that's what he would do every weekend, and he'd walked all over Derbyshire. I also recall, even at that young age, them mentioning he was not married, emphasising that this was by choice. I don't think I was left with some subconscious fear that walkers have to be single or would become so as a result of pursuing this activity, no, I'm sure that has never concerned me. I do think, however, there is a place of solitude that can be experienced when walking and, I can now say, I fully understand why someone would want to walk alone.

During my school days, when I was at Victoria Road Infants School in Chester, I recall we had a teacher from Wales called Mr Morris. He used to talk about his weekend walks over Moel Fammau, a mountain in Wales over two thousand feet high! To me, a mere infant, this sounded high and captivated my imagination—a challenge for the future!?

It was a few years later, we'd moved house again but that's another story, and I could see Moel Fammau on the horizon from my bedroom window. Whether there was some subconscious connection at the time or not I wouldn't like to speculate, anyhow the reasons that instigated this next episode of strange behaviour have become lost over time. On the occasional Saturday morning my dad was persuaded to drop me off, with one or two intrepid or equally foolish school mates, at a place called Cilcain, one side of Moel Fammau. We'd spend the day walking up and over the top then down the other side where dad would meet us in the car at Loggerheads. I presumed that he'd arranged his working day so that he would be passing at about the right time. If you're thinking mobile phones or any other means of communication forget it, I'm going back in time here. It was always the same one or two mates and we are still in touch today. What other like minded behaviour results in such bonding I wonder?

These excursions continued for several years and, looking back now, I have to say that the most memorable of these took place in winter. Mother would always make a flask of hot soup to accompany us to the top; I recall a low cost Army and Navy Stores rucksack on my back with the flask, a chocolate bar and a bag of crisps in it. We would attempt to picnic, our frozen fingers struggling to manipulate the cup of hot drink in the freezing blizzard as we sheltered behind a stone wall of the derelict monument on top of the hill.

Only occasionally do I recall seeing another wanderer, especially in the winter months. Strangely perhaps, as I look back now, I wonder if that was one of the attractions I found in doing it? I think so . . . . to do something no one else was doing . . . . well something the majority of other school kids my age were not doing, well, alright then, something the majority of any age group were not doing!

The memory of the painful fingers and toes seemed to fade rapidly once the journey was accomplished and, however a reality they must have been at the time, I now have no painful recollection of them at all. Yes, winter was most memorable; it would sometimes be dark before we arrived in Loggerheads so it must have been a long and challenging walk for us. Without fail dad was always waiting. I'll never know why dad went along with it, did he suffer it, did he hope it was a passing phase that would soon fizzle out, or was he just being dad. I think I'll categorise it as encouragement. I remember wearing the same shoes I went to school in, no desires or even thoughts about walking boots. Would they have helped? I'd like to think they may have even detracted from the recklessness and pleasures of this school boy escapade.

One summer I managed to persuade my mates we should cycle it, up and over the top on our bikes and back again, a round distance of 36 miles. Another one of those unforgettable events, my bike was so shaken when cycling down the mountain the handlebars broke off, and what else can you do at that moment but laugh. Who cared about that, we were having an adventure, me and my mates cycling over Moel Fammau over forty years ago. I'd never heard or seen anyone doing it so I'd like to think it was a first. I'm also talking about your standard pushbike of forty years ago not these hi tech modern day bikes with shock absorbers, disc brakes and mud tyres. Anyhow, we did it, and as we shot down the very long steep hill from Loggerheads I can still hear Tony shouting "30", "40", then "50!" with reference to our speed, he had the bike with a Speedo fitted. You probably have to form a queue to do that today.

Snowdon was now in my sights but I realised it commanded some respect and I'd need real walking boots. It's been many years since my last ascent but I keep meaning to go back, there's a great pub at Plas y Gurid that deserves a visit. One year, for no know reason, my old mate from uni suggested we walk Pen-y-Ghent. I mean I'd been on several Lake District holidays and rambled about a bit, like most I suppose, but this had a special appeal to me, something enchanting even. Perhaps it was that there were fewer people, or perhaps I'd reached an age where I could appreciate, or experience, something extra that I hadn't previously realised was available when walking. I've stomped up those three peaks: Pen-y-Ghent, Whernside and Ingelborough many times over the years and they still remain a passionate favourite of mine.

I have to mention the wife at this point. Soon after we met one of my first objectives was to discard her 20 year old boots, which she gracefully accepted should be replaced, and we did so with a fine pair of Brasher walking boots. The next weekend I took her up the three peaks to try them out in anger. We were the only tent in the campsite on a very frosty February morning! The second time we camped in rain so heavy we couldn't have a conversation, never mind sleep, for the noise. Looking back it could be said she was thrown in the deep end, sorry about that my love.

Let me be clear that these forays, which some of you would like to term expeditions (it all depends on your ability) were not frequent affairs, by most standards far from it. Fifteen years later, the year prior to our big walk, we found ourselves having a fine week in the Lakes. I climbed Skiddaw twice and we also managed to fit in Haystacks and Buttermere. I have to say, given that we have office jobs, we were pleasantly surprised at our level of fitness, I can only attribute that to many years of dog walking.

So, circumstances being favourable; time allowed off work, sufficient funds, feeling capable, the challenge itself, all convincing us that the time in life had come to grasp the opportunity which had finally presented itself. We should head off to St Bees and start walking to Robin Hoods Bay. No problem.

As in most of these cases the decision was a seemingly easy and painless one, the consequences would no doubt unfold as the departure time drew nearer. Camping was not going to be an option, that was for bygone days, at our time of life this was going to be an occasion for B&Bs and the Sherpa van to transport the overnight luggage. Anyway I wouldn't expect the wife to lug all those heavy bags all that way! A preferred date was chosen along with the route, the number of nights and the B&Bs, and without much thought the Internet button was pressed. Start Date 1st September 2010.

There was the usual expectation, the one we generally experience when looking forward to our annual holiday, until a package arrived in the post. I opened it glanced at the contents and, seeing there was far too much detail to be bothered with, placed it in the bookcase. For many weeks it remain there, although we knew what it was, there was a reluctance to find out what we had actually let ourselves in for, fearful that we had made some impromptu decision we might regret.

Eventually the time came so, one evening, we sat down with the Maps, Guide Book, and a bottle of wine, to peruse the itinerary and examine our route in detail. Our holiday was a 200 mile walk, day one was fifteen miles, day two was even further, with the option of climbing Haystacks thrown in for good measure, and after several hours and a second bottle of wine we paused on day three realising this was going to be a walk like no other we'd done. Day three looked strange, only half the distance of day two but took the same time to walk it, then it suddenly registered; we were going over some serious hills. I found some comfort knowing we chosen the soft option, which was to do the twenty five mile, or more, stages over two days instead of one, it was suppose to be a holiday after all.

We spent many evenings and bottles of wine to help digest the challenge that lie before us. It was clear we needed to buy some proper clothes and serious weather gear but we needed a daily walking Plan to get us fit. To accomplish this we spent ten minutes devising a chart which we would fill in every day after every walk and we hung it in a prominent position on the kitchen wall, this would be our key fitness performance indicator. Starting out with a mere five miles a day the target was to increase the distance over a couple of months to achieve a comfortable 15 miles, thus ensuring we would reach the required level of fitness just before the start.

A few weeks before departure we did a 17 mile walk and concluded we were ready, no problem.

Chapter 1

And so to chapter one, or rather day one, of our fifteen day voyage of discovery commencing with the train journey to St Bees. It has to be mentioned, as the train journey to St Bees was itself quite enlightening, helping to leave daily life behind and look forward to what lie ahead. The trip to Carlisle could be said to be as one might expect a train journey to be, by modern standards, but the coast line train from Carlisle to St Bees was a reminder that times in those parts had seen far better days. It's not that the folks still live in, what some would consider to be, a bygone era but as an engineer I can't help feeling depressed when I see industrial decline. The train was still providing a vital service to the local community, and the occasional foreign traveller like me. At this point, I couldn't help observing the occupants. It was mid week and our carriage was about half full, the occupants fell into two main categories; either returning home from shopping in Carlisle or they were returning from School, which left me wondering where all the other walkers I expected might be. On a selfish note I was hoping there would not be a great number, I would hate to think we'd have to queue over every stile. Other than the frequent bellowing of "tickets please" from the female ticket collector I was starting to relax and enjoy the journey. Travelling from Aspatria to Maryport, which as a port dates back 2000 to Roman times, on the railway George Stevenson put in to export coal to Ireland, then through Flimby and on to Workington I was beginning to feel nostalgic. I was surprised that the scars of the quarries, iron works and collieries still remained to serve as a reminder of just how industrious we once were and that nature had not yet healed the wounds. Sadly, as I looked to the land, I could only conclude that our struggle with the earth had left only melancholy in the air. In contrast the view out to sea bared no scars, slowly turning to a colourful sunset as the train chugged along the meandering coastline on to Harrington, Parton, and Whitehaven before finally arriving at St Bees.

From now on we were on foot, bags in tow as they had little wheels on, and our first navigational challenge was to find Abbey Farm House B&B. Although I was not feeling weary it had been a longish day and after all that relaxing, finally finding myself stood outside St Bees railway station, trying to suddenly engage my brain to studying maps and read the directions in order to orientate ourselves came as a surprise which, quite simply, failed and led to more confusion. After five minutes we put the maps away followed our nose and, as if by surprise, there it was. What a corker of a place, if all the accommodation was going to be of this standard for the whole journey we would be spoilt and I would also be surprised. It was spotless with en suite bathroom, our own lounge with TV, tea making facilities, bottles of water, biscuits, all within a very old charming building on a quite backwater you would happily recommend to your boss. After a while we were fully installed, our thoughts then turned, naturally I would like to think, to food. So, what else could we do that evening but to go for a walk and find a pub! St Bees also deserved a look at so, with the help of lady of the house, we devised a circular route to take in all St Bees had to offer, heading first to the beach to enjoy the remaining evening light. Looking West across the Irish Sea toward the Isle of Mann, whilst strolling on an empty sandy beach, we witnessed the close of the day. My camera was purposely to hand and its first job was to capture this beautiful evening sky as it changed colour. The time felt right to stick a toe in the water, and photograph that too, on order to mark the beginning of our journey, rather than wait until morning and, as tradition has it, pick up a pebble for company on the way. We then strolled south stumbling along a very stony beach, aware that straining an ankle at this point would be curtains as well as stupid, but spirits were high fuelled by the many months of preparation and realisation that this was it. After a mile or so we turned back towards St Bees, leaving the beach and passing under a tiny railway tunnel to find ourselves on the high street and heading back to the sleepy "town" centre. Given a choice of only a couple of pubs we singled out the Queens Hotel as the place to eat and drink, simply because from the outside it looked the most inviting, and without much deliberation, went directly in to find it was absolutely packed. Given that we'd completely explored St Bees and found few other choices we patiently queued to order food. I then made a conscious effort to adopt a holiday mood deciding to relax, helped with a pint at the bar, whilst we patiently and joyfully waited for a table to come free. Unlike the people on the train I couldn't help notice the numerous fit and healthy looking customers in the pub who were all wearing outdoor gear, a description not befitting ourselves I hasten to add, unwittingly we'd obviously arrived at the launching pad. The patient waiting paid dividends, the food was quality and the beer hit the spot too, we were fuelled and ready. The only thought left in my mind was—would I be able to go to bed and sleep that night or would the excitement of the adventure and challenges that lie ahead prevent me from doing so?

The next morning after a good nights sleep, undoubtedly helped by the requisite number of pints in the Queens, I woke feeling unbelievably enthusiastic and immediately got up and took a shower keen to ensure everything was ready so we could be on our way as agreed and planned by, whatever the circumstances, no later than, 8.30am. Finding the dining room was as easy as finding the B&B and we sat down for breakfast, completely alone, at a table by a little window which overlooked the Church Yard and School Cricket Green. After a while a door opened and a lady wearing a white frock and a smile approached asking what we would like to eat. A wonderful smell of things cooking had followed her through the door, it was a combination of bacon, sausage and coffee, but our plan was to eat carbohydrates to provide long term energy, like eggs on toast, rather than the fatty but extremely tempting 'Full English' option. Somehow my wife knew what I was thinking and glanced in my direction to ensure I made the correct choice. The lady left with our order and, as we sat quietly, I could hear it being prepared. The food was exactly what we needed to start our day and, just as we were done, one other couple arrived for their breakfast, so I said "good morning". It didn't look to me like they were about to set off walking and they chose to sit as far away as possible. Other than returning "good morning", there were no facial expressions exchanged between us which would have instigated a conversation and that seemed to be the entire complement of the B&B. It left me feeling a bit sad.

Talking to our landlady in passing, for some reason feeling obliged to do so, she managed to make a short story long and told us the tale of how she met her husband on the coast to coast walk ten years ago. They then decided to move to St Bees and run a B&B and how she now meets all different kinds of people etc etc. "Interesting" I thought but inwardly hoping I wouldn't suffer the same fate—running a B&B that is, I already had a wife! Unstoppable she continued to recount all sorts of tales about the people who had started their walk from her B&B, ending her tale with some lady who had planned to walk the Coast to Coast route in just eight days and was never heard from again, which was not the best thought to leave me with. Thankfully she realised she had to prepare our packed lunches and left us to do our own packing.

As instructed we left our bags in the main doorway, ready for collection by the Sherpa Van Company, and with a "good bye" and sincere "thank you" grabbed our packed lunch, strapped ourselves into our rucksacks and, while still feeling optimistic, eagerly set off heading west, destination the Shepherds Arms, Ennerdale Bridge, distance 15 miles.

During the short walk to the coast I was more occupied performing a mental check list than observing the scenery, a sort of pre-flight checklist, grasping the occasional moment as each box was ticked, for a farewell glance backwards. At the seashore the camera came out for the mandatory photo of us standing in front of the "start of the coast to coast walk" signpost. There was no one around, thankfully, so I held the camera at arms length pointing it back at ourselves as we stood there smiling confidently, after all it was a beautiful day and we couldn't have wished for better weather on day one. It was a brief pause in the scheme of things, but I decided the last one for a while, and packed the camera firmly away, mentally, physically, and spiritually I was now ready to start my journey. I looked north to see the path revealed before us, as a line cut through the grass by many feet, rising steeply then following the cliff edge until it disappeared on the horizon. I took a deep breath—we were off!!

St Bees had the last word as I clapped eyes on a Fleet of holiday caravans, nestled at the foot of the cliff and all painted greenhouse green, presumably an attempt to blend them into the landscape, a good idea but, sadly, a poor result. "I wonder if that should be a Camel", I said to Deborah, "rather than Fleet, on the basis that Caravan is the collective noun for Camels"? She looked inquisitively as I waited for a response when I was suddenly startled as a ball bounced right in front of us, which stopped us in our tracks. I turned so see a little dog running like mad after it, reminding me we had put our two dogs in kennels. There was an old chap in a long coat approaching and, feeling in high spirits, I exclaimed "Good Morning" which was well received and we exchanged a few pleasantries. We set off again, I hoped that was the last interruption, the time had come to focus on the task ahead and no more was said as we started to climb the cliff top to walk along the coastal path finally leaving St Bees and its inhabitants behind.

Music: Vivaldi's Spring from the four seasons reflects the enthusiastic start to our journey.

Confidence was high having, somewhat effortlessly, climbed to the cliff tops. Strolling along looking out to sea I returned to the conversation about the collective noun for caravans, in an attempt to both explore and seek closure on the matter, but to no avail so I dropped it assuming Deborah had other things on her mind. Two hundred miles lay ahead of us and I didn't know what to feel. On a practical note I thought we had everything we'd need, in our rucksacks were maps, guide book, camera, water proofs for the bad weather which would no doubt come, an extra pair of dry socks, water bottles, packed lunch from the B&B, torch, Swiss army pen knife, string, bog paper, and a brand of plasters as recommended by Nicola which I hoped we wouldn't need. Mentally, however, I'd just realised I had no idea what I should have prepared for, like other major events in life that we simply can not prepare for such as going to School for the first time, starting a new job, falling in love, getting married. Believing it's going to take care of what's to come we spend money on insurance policies, sold to us for all sorts of reasons, believe me it's not. Another alternative is to try and avoid the event, the first day I was sent to school I ran off, but you'll only postpone it.

A few hundred yards ahead of us we could see two chaps with large rucksacks and, as the path levelled off, another couple in the distance ahead of them. I concluded they must all be doing the Coast to Coast walk, we would not be on our own. I couldn't see anyone behind us and we became comfortable going at our own steady pace, neither gaining or loosing on those in front, just having our own conversation and stopping now and then to adjust a boot lace or take the camera out to capture the moment for prosperity, things had got off to a good start, seriously I was feeling confident about this. I glanced back now and then and finally noticed a young lass with her dog rapidly gaining on us, at the same time the two chaps in front of us had stopped for some unknown reason and we would soon be getting close enough to exchange words.

I was uncertain what to say to them, these would be the first people we'd meet who were also on the same journey as ourselves, they appeared to have all the right gear and looked like they were in their natural environment and I began to wonder what they'd think of us. Perhaps they might they think we were stupid attempting this journey, no matter, it wouldn't be right to walk by without saying anything. I started to slow down as we approached but conversation wasn't much more than "hello" and a few words about our location relative to a Lighthouse which, thankfully, I'd noted on the map earlier and threw into the conversation to suggest I had some local knowledge. In a laid back casual and dismissive sort of way, as if I'd asked a stranger in the High Street, they said the Lighthouse should appear on our right in about a mile so we picked up the pace again and carried on walking.

When I glanced back again I could see the young lass was right on the sea front playing with her dog in an isolated cove, I could see her throwing something for the dog to swim out to, what a delight I thought, presuming she knew exactly what she was doing and wouldn't get trapped by the tide. Another ten minutes and the lighthouse duly appeared in sight but rather than stop to investigate, like a tourist might, we continued walking. When I next looked back at the Lighthouse I noticed that the two chaps, who were now following fairly close behind us, were heading directly towards the Lighthouse to take a closer look. That caused us to stop and debate whether we might have missed something and should to do the same, but I felt we didn't have the time to explore monuments, I saw the two chaps sit down outside the lighthouse, presumably for 11es, but eating was also still too early for me so we agreed to press on.

At the headland we finally turned to the east, clearly there was no choice, and the Lakeland Fells came into view. According to the guide book we were about to come across a bench, where one could sit looking out to sea, which was supposedly the loneliest seat on the Coast to Coast path.

It did invite the question who would go to the trouble of putting a seat in the middle of nowhere and why, and to be honest with you I have no idea. Soon enough we came across the other couple we'd seen ahead of us who had also stopped for elevenses and were sitting on it. As we were the only beings for miles around it seemed appropriate to stop and say hello, and be prepared to take time to converse if necessary, the seat being an obvious conversation starter.

Taking a pebble from the Irish Sea at St Bees

Sat on the loneliest bench were David and Caroline were from Australia, slightly older than us I'd like to think, certainly not yet retired and were taking a 3 month sabbatical. This walk was one of their ambitions which they wanted to fulfil whilst touring Europe and visiting some relatives in the England. After several minutes, with some slight hesitation, but still chatting we all started walking together, Deborah and Caroline doing most of the talking. At last we were pointing in the right direction and heading due East, which made me feel more comfortable if leaving me puzzled why we'd walked so many miles north and up the coastline before doing so. This was something I'd have to figure out but, for now, I was content to leave that question unanswered until later.

The conversation had turned out to be a pleasant distraction, we'd been going for half an hour or so without having to think hard about where we were heading or look at the maps, but I'd had the guide book in one hand open at the relevant page and I noticed David had done the same. Coming to a clearing among the trees I could see the fells in the distance, this time appearing as a dark jagged silhouette against a clear sky, I paused to look. "That's where we're heading" I affirmed with our Antipodean companions, we all stopped for a moment to gaze at the Fells ahead which also halted our conversation, the silence was something I welcomed.

Music of Also Sprach Zarathustra Opus 30 by Richard Strauss would set the mood.

It wasn't long after that we, our little party of four that is, arrived in Sandwich the first village on our journey. Unfortunately there wasn't much to interest us and, thanks to the good guide book, we navigated our way through it effortlessly heading for the next villages, Moor Row then Cleator. The distance we'd walked, and the time taken, to get to the main road near Sandwith seemed to have a pointless irony as it was much further by miles than the signpost, defiantly pointing back to St Bees, indicated. I laughed to myself, how often is life like that I thought; we set off and our paths lead us back to where we started, having taken a lot of effort to get there! When we look back there was clearly a much easier way, so what's the lesson? Is the destination more important than the route we take to get there, or is what we learn on our route more important than the destination?

I'm sure none of our little party felt obliged to stay together, conversation was polite and even informative at times but not incessant, I for one was happy to carry on. It began to dawn on me that our time together was also building our self confidence and perhaps that would help with the mental preparation we all needed for the long journey ahead. Approaching Moor Row, however, I realised we'd taken a wrong turn and wondered if this would be a test of leadership. I stopped and announced we were on the wrong side of the stream, "beck" in these parts, whereas David expressed his certainty that we were doing the right thing following this old wall which was referenced on his map. There was a moment of silence while everyone gave it some thought, I don't think David was convinced we'd gone wrong but within a minute he and Caroline agreed to turn back. Thankfully, about a mile later, it was very clear that we'd found the old wall referenced in his guide book, it was twelve foot high and looked like it was built by monks, so everyone was happy we were back on track. Sometimes we have to agree to work together, whoever we find ourselves with, to the benefit of all. That was something else I hadn't thought of as a requirement on this journey, Teamwork!

Cleator had a pub and a shop, I admit I hadn't done my homework and didn't find that out until we actually arrived there. It was far too dangerous to enter the pub so early in the day and having no need for provisions Deborah and I passed by the village shop too. As we did so I noticed a few other walkers in the shop, they must have set off knowing it would be open and provide them with lunch, David and Caroline were tempted to make use of it and went in so we decided the time had come to part company. Deborah and I strolled on to look for a quiet spot all to ourselves, where we could stop and eat our packed lunch, and more importantly find a place to pee, knowing that the next leg of the journey would be an hour's sweaty climb up Dent Hill.

Just as the gradient started to increase we found an idyllic spot by a beck, off came my boots and socks and there I was dangling my feet in the cold running water while sitting on a branch overhanging the stream and munching the pre packed fodder. I have to say very welcome it was too; the lady in our B&B had packed frozen orange juice which had just thawed out and was now the perfect refreshment. Had I been thirsty I would have filled the water bottles from the stream it looked that good but, having already put my feet in it, I resisted. Taking plenty of time to let my feet dry naturally I put on clean socks and, feeling completely refreshed, was ready to tackle our first real climb, Dent Hill.

As it turned out the climb up Dent Hill wasn't so bad. Deborah and I were on our own again and making good progress plodding along nicely. Deborah shared with me some of the conversation she had had with Caroline, who'd apparently just finished a course of chemotherapy so this walk was a personal challenge as well as something she'd set her heart on doing a long while ago. I was thinking about her situation, but didn't want to try and imagine myself in her shoes, then, surprisingly, we arrived at the summit to find David and Caroline plus the two chaps we met earlier in the day having all stopped for a rest. They must have all walked quietly past us while we were having lunch back at the beck. Each of the two chaps had a huge rucksack on his back as they were carrying absolutely everything and were discussing where to camp that night. One of them had done the walk four times before but the other, quite a young looking chap, indicated it was his first attempt and despite the physical training he was struggling a bit, I would have been too with all that weight on my back. Now a party of six we set off all together exchanging words, the chap who'd walked it 4 times keen to recount some of his past episodes.

Ravens Crag had been mentioned several times on route and as we arrived I could see there was a significant decent, this put a lot of strain on parts of the legs that don't often get such exercise. It was every man for himself, my approach was to traverse it like I would skiing down a steep slope, some had quite a different technique giving us all different rates of decent. At the bottom we all gathered and looked back up the slope waiting for our jelly-like knees to set, that was the steepest decent on the whole journey. The route then turned into a pleasant but very long hike following the wonderfully named Nannycatch Beck which led all the way to Ennerdale Bridge. It was now gone 5 o'clock, David and Caroline were not staying at the same pub we were, and for some reason Deborah and I pushed on leaving the others behind as if time was running out. Something else we had underestimated, blamed at the time on the hot weather, was the amount of water we had carried, both our water bottles were now completely dry, and I was thirsty.

Our arrival in Ennerdale Bridge came as a great relief, our day one milestone successfully accomplished, not bad, I thought, given the training schedule we'd set ourselves. At first glance the old pub, our bed for the night, looked quite picturesque so we eagerly entered the lobby to see both our bags among a pile of similar luggage on the floor, there was no one about although I could hear muffled dialogue coming from what I thought was the kitchen. We waited for some considerable time before a lady arrived clearly agitated. We were welcomed, ish, and told we were on the first floor, a key attached to a house brick was thrust into my hand and we were left to struggle up the winding staircase with our luggage by ourselves. Our room looked like it was last decorated in the 1930s and contained the same dark walnut furniture my mum and dad had when they got married and I grew up with, probably because it was built to last forever. The main problem with the room was space, the old bed and wardrobe now completely filled the room, which had also shrunk due to the addition of the modern en suite facility, circa 1980, in a poor attempt to keep up with the times. Deborah went to sit on the bed and sure enough a spring made a classic "boing" sound causing us both to laugh loudly. The en suit was not shall we say spacious, I'm not a tall chap but when I sat on the toilet my feet were in the shower which could best be described as a drizzle as I found out when I came to use it. However, there was a sink and hot water, ideal for washing socks in, a bare necessity in any Hotel room after a days walking.

My plan was to have three pairs of socks in a rotating system, one pair on, one pair ready to put on, and one pair in the wash. The bedroom sash window, overlooking the beer garden, formed a perfect clothesline located in a warm drying breeze. So successful was the laundry the plan immediately expanded to include shirts and knickers convinced they would be dry in the morning.

I had suspected it for some time, just after the decent of Ravens Crag, and sure enough a close examination of the ball of my left foot revealed a blister. Pushing on for the last few miles that day had been a mistake, I was annoyed with myself, struggling to understand how it had happened or what I'd done wrong, especially as I was wearing these new fantastic 1000 mile no blister guarantee socks! Too late to send those back and ask for a refund. Determined this inconvenience would not prevent me from walking the following day, we went for a short stroll to explore the pretty little village, my left foot was so sore we didn't go far before I turned back still uttering in annoyance. By habit I reached for my phone only then to realise there was no reception, hence no communication. I normally phoned my mum at the same time every day to check she was alright but there was nothing I could about it or desperately wanted to, perhaps it was a blessing.

It seemed a good time to find our Hotel bar so we bought a pint of the local brew and went to sit outside in the beer garden. Strange no one else was out there I thought, as it was such a beautiful evening. There was a pretty small stream, beck, that ran along the bottom of the beer garden, a lovely place to sit and enjoy a drink one would think, but my bum had hardly touched the seat when the wife and I stared directly at one another. Words were not needed to communicate and the lack of oxygen to her face meant a hasty retreat back to the bar was in order. Blimey, as I drew breath and realised our mistake, you can only experience this smell if you've lived in a house with a cess pit when it's in the process of being emptied. We tried to make our retreat look graceful and I wondered if the people in the bar had placed bets on how long we would stay outdoors.

We sat at a table in the bar, pushing the menu aside, wondering what to talk about. There was no background music and no carpet so every sound could be heard. Out of the few people in the bar most, from their dress and weathered skin, were clearly doing the walk, but it was a mystery why we hadn't seen them at anytime during the day. After downing a pint we deliberated over the menu deciding to err on the side of caution and plump for chicken and chips. I heard a couple of older chaps conversing behind me and another couple, about our age who were in full view, talking with what sounded like an American accent. When he went to the bar I was suddenly struck by his question to the bar maid, which I couldn't help overhearing, he asked whether the beer was pasteurised? Clearly he was not a real ale connoisseur and I felt tempted to butt into the conversation to enlighten him but stopped short, waiting for the perplexed bar maid to deliver her answer and wondering what horrible disease a pint of real ale might give him.

We kept the evening to ourselves, washed a mediocre chicken and chips down with a couple more pints then, due to the onset of weariness, turned in for the night reflecting on the events that day and deciding what shape plaster would best cover my blistered foot so I could keep walking.

If I were as lonely as that seat I can see how it might be tempting to leap off the cliff, some people can be that lonely even when others are very near. It's good to be alone sometimes to find out, and be, who we are, but not good to feel lonely. I'd like to return to that seat one day by myself to experience the isolation for a while.

View from the lonely seat

Chapter 2

I opened my eyes to see my socks and pants hanging over the sash window, a stark reminder of where I was and what I was doing here, and then beyond to see a beautiful sky telling me this was going to be another wonderful day. I was surprised I'd had such a good nights sleep, due no doubt to the beer and exercise. We'd been blessed with two consecutive days of good weather, very unusual in these parts, statistically they can have more rain here in a day than the rest of the UK in a year, the guide book emphasising the need to be quipped with good waterproofs. Today we were offered a choice of route; we could accept the challenge to climb and follow the ridge to Haystacks, adding another arduous couple of hours to the 15 mile hike ahead of us, or keep to the less strenuous lower route. Wishing to appear democratic I ran the two options past Deborah, although my mind was already made up, I was going to be nursing the blister on my left foot so an early start and a steady pace would be the order of the day.

Motivated by the good weather and a desire to move on, as much as leave this place behind, we were eager enough to be the first couple to locate the dining room where we were greeted by a musty damp smell, possibly an attestation to the rain fall combined with last nights stale food, certainly not appetising. Not long afterwards the American couple arrived, came in, looked around, and sat down at the nearest table. We all exchanged "Good Morning" I managed to force a smile but was actually feeling embarrassed about the quality of our English hospitality. I decided to remain quite rather than attempt conversation that might involve breathing up my nose. Within ten minutes there were nine of us sat waiting for breakfast, all eager to depart, and then a young giggly apologising waitress with fizzy hair dashed in, hastily took all our orders, and left again returning much later, less stressed, to serve our eggs on toast and a pot of tea. An older chap, who was sat on his own, I'd seen and heard him talking in the bar to someone last night, asked the waitress to fill his water bottles from the tap, pointing out that he had in fact put purifying tablets in the bottles. I smiled, wondering if she would think he was actually trying to make a statement about the cess pit stench, but she simply did what he asked and returned showing no emotion. This served to remind me that we ran out of water yesterday, our two water bottles being inadequate for our daily needs, so we decided to pack a couple of plastic bottles of water as well.

As we left the dining room the waitress told us to collect our packed lunches from the kitchen hatch, ordered and paid for the previous evening. I identified our packed lunch at the bottom of a heap by our room number, our food appeared to have been treated with the same contempt as our luggage so I deduced both had been dealt with by the same member of staff. After dropping off the key and overnight bags exactly where we found them we set off, at a cautious pace, stopping every few hundred yards to retighten my boot laces trying to ensure there would be no rubbing that would aggravate my swore foot.

Ennerdale Water was indeed a beautiful sight, the water was like a mile wide mirror, reflecting the early morning light, a camera moment, and we were the only ones there. We stood looking at the view for some time before two Australian ladies arrived. They seemed genuinely appreciative of the landscape and having said a polite "Good Morning" also decided to take some pictures. I could then hear more people arriving and decided we should quickly move on, our destination today was Stonethwaite Farm, Borrowdale, about 16 or 17 miles.

The path along the Lake shore seemed to go on forever, just five miles according to the map, but it was rocky, uneven under foot, and not like one might expect walking along a lake "shore" to be or wished for today, however the mole skin plaster was doing a great job and I was so pleased I could walk without my foot being a constant irritation to both myself and Deborah. After a few miles we stopped again to gaze at the fantastic view across the lake, Ennerdale Water, which mirrored the mountains and sky. The complete peace and quite was then surprisingly broken by the sound of a Kookaburra echoing around the lake, a very good imitation I have to say, what better way to announce you're from Australia? I was pleased someone else was enjoying their day but thankful too, after the third time, that no one had responded in fear that this calling might escalate among our Kookaburra calling cousins.

Jumping over a stile we nearly descended on top of the American couple, the ones who were at breakfast that morning, both sat on a log examining their guidebook. He seemed eager to engage in conversation, so we stopped and did the formal introductions. Peter and Brenda announced they were from British Columbia, immediately making me feel ignorant at accent identification but I'd got away with it. Peter, playing the humorous type, insisted that they'd stopped because it was his wife who'd got "tuckered" so he had to rest too and keep her company. I couldn't help notice they had one tiny rucksack and trainers on their feet which gave me a bad feeling they were under prepared. The only contribution Brenda made to the conversation was reference to a swarm of flying ants that plagued them at the top of Dent Hill yesterday and asked if we'd suffered the same fate. I started to say I hadn't heard anyone mention a Swarm of Ants and then began to wonder if they might have walked over a different Hill. Peter inquired about the Black Sail Hut, a remote youth hostel on route, asking if there would be lunch available! This confirmed my fears, it turned out they had no food whatsoever, so we felt obliged to leave them with a chocolate bar each and then walked on saying "see you later".

I was really starting to enjoy the solitude on this journey, thinking we were making good progress, when we were suddenly overtaken by an old chap wearing a white outfit who came marching past us at a rate of knots. He looked to me like he was in his seventies, he just had time to say he had to go fast on the flat as he couldn't go up hills quick and we would most likely catch him up later, then he was gone before either of us had time to think of a suitable response.

Just before we reached the end of the lake, where the river ran into it, we chose a place to stop to look at the scenery, check the map, and rest for a while. It felt like elevenses to my belly although I really had no idea of the time. Within ten minutes everyone we'd spoken to that morning, followed by David and Caroline, passed by and seeing that we were tucking into a sandwich simply smiled, said hello and left us in peace. At first I thought it seemed natural good manners to leave people grazing on their own, but their facial expressions said more than that, I was witnessing the development of camaraderie, something that normally took months, or years, was happening in days and even hours. Empathy?

A brief snack was sufficient to restore our energy levels and we set off with renewed enthusiasm to see Peter and Brenda just a few hundred yards ahead walking slowly, Peters' head stuck firmly in his guidebook clearly deliberating the way ahead. As we got nearer I realised I was wrong, it wasn't a small rucksack he was carrying, but just a shoulder bag. I was genuinely concerned thinking they were ill prepared for this journey and might wonder off aimlessly never to be seen again. I said "hello again" and his head popped up, as if slightly startled, I said we need to cross the river here for the path to the Black Sail Hut at which he said they would go this way, pointing to the opposite bank of the river, in a determined voice, suggesting his choice of route must be the right one and set off, Brenda too.

I couldn't allow them to wonder for miles up the wrong side of the valley so, being certain of our position, called out "I'll show you on my map" reaching into my pocket to produce it. At this he immediately stopped and retorted "MAP?!" simultaneously turning his head from side to side expressing surprise while walking slowly backwards. I admit I was stunned for a few moments by his acting, concluding that this guy must be trying to wind me up. Anyhow he finally looked at my map and changed his mind, Brenda dutifully followed him without saying a word, I couldn't believe they didn't have a map or lunch. After we all crossed the river, via a wide stretch of boggy ground didn't look like the correct route either, our path joined a dusty lane, pleasing at first because it was more even under foot, but a gruelling relentless ascent that went on mile after mile. We hadn't exchanged many words with the Canadian couple, his earlier enthusiasm for conversation seem to have dried up. With still four miles to go to Black Sail Hut we came to a hostel, without so much as a "good bye" Brenda headed straight for it and Peter followed her, I presume she was looking for lunch.

Deborah and I plodded on to arrive at Black Sail Hut where everyone we'd met on route in the last two days, plus a dozen others, were seated on a rock, or the grass, eating their lunch admiring the views. I'd diligently studied the Guide Book the night before and, apparently, you can arrange to stay the night in Black Sail Hut. I have to say it's an amazing location; any one passing by is welcome to help themselves and make a cup of tea, so Deborah did just that. Unable to find an unoccupied proper seat anywhere we too sat on the grass to be joined by three Herdwick sheep looking like they were waiting to be offered a sandwich. We weren't short of food and had accumulated more chocolate bars than we could possibly eat, I'd kept stashing them away just in case, in case of what? I don't know, just in case. There was a couple who we hadn't seen before and they'd brought their dog with them, which surprised me, the dog looked a bit stressed out but, being a collie, I presumed it would have the stamina to walk all day every day. I heard the old chap in the white outfit, who sped past us earlier, asking if anyone had any blisters and wanted a plaster, I noticed at least one taker, Caroline. I didn't need reminding of my blister, my socks were already off to let my feet breathe, I figured keeping them dry should reduce any further rubbing. I also figured Black Sail Hut was about half distance today but, all things considered, we'd made reasonably good time and were keeping up with others who did this sort of thing regularly, or looked like they did.

Lying in the grass, with the sheep, in this idyllic location on such a beautiful day made it tempting to stay put rather than start walking again, so I decided more time for mental and physical preparation was required before I would put my socks back on, especially as the path from Black Sail Hut looked like it went a mile vertically upwards. When I finally stood up, orientating myself with true vertical and horizontal, I saw that the path did go straight upwards so I strapped myself onto the rucksack in preparation for some rock climbing. Sure enough, just as I anticipated, the path duly turned into a rocky ascent and we found ourselves climbing up a stairway of huge stones, which also happened to be the route a beck had chosen to come down the hill, creating mini waterfalls, making the wet rocks slippery to walk on and generally adding to the fun of it all. For the first time I could feel my heart pounding and the blood rushing around my body, the route was blindingly obvious, so it was a case of head down, look for foot holds and keep going.

About half way up, just as he said it would happen, we met the old chap who had sped past us earlier, the same who was handing out plasters. It was a welcome excuse to take a rest and wait for the wife to catch up. Jack, ex Army and lifelong Rambling Club member, was doing this for charity with his mate, who we hadn't met yet because he was some way ahead. He was debating whether to fill his water bottle from the beck, if we were above 2000 feet he reckoned it was ok to drink, unless there was a dead sheep in it we didn't know about of course. We weren't tempted with a refill but stayed to observe the views and long enough for my pulse rate to drop into double figures, finally leaving Jack to make his own way up. I was wondering if his white outfit doubled as an oxygen tent. At the summit there was a solitary tall thin figure I presumed to be his walking companion who, looking slightly sorrowful, confirmed it by saying "he can't do the hills anymore", his body language didn't imply he wanted to engage in any further conversation with me so I carried on without stopping.

Having climbed it the previous year I knew we were just below the summit of Haystacks and therefore, thinking I knew better, started to relying on instinct to find my way rather than looking at the map. However, I became a bit disoriented and consequently we wasted several valuable minutes finding the right path, which was all my fault and I apologised. The Australian ladies, who we'd met at the beginning of the day by the Ennerdale Water, being a bit younger and fitter were gradually catching us up, so taking an interest in what inspired them to take on this challenge we walked and talked together for a while on our way down from Haystacks. Of all the people we'd spoken to that day no one had ever been to Stonethwaite accept Jack, who told us that the nearby pub did good food. That thought was enough to keep my spirits up on what was becoming a very long day on a sore foot. A Slate Quarry was not on my "to do" list but I took advantage of it and sat down outside the Visitors Centre while Deborah went in to purchase two ice creams, soon to be followed by the Australian couple, then the couple with the dog, which also looked like it needed refreshment and a well earned rest.

From the outset we both knew today was going to be one of the longest days on our walk, I didn't think I'd be nursing a blister but was thankful it was bearable and so far hadn't caused me to abandon my journey although that thought had crossed my mind. There was still a long way to go, thankfully all down hill, but nowhere to escape the heat of the afternoon sun, this is when we realised that bringing sun cream might have been a good idea, another item overlooked. After the experience of the previous day's hike we'd made a point of resting more often, dare I say we'd even been sensible, and we'd taken twice the amount of water as we had on the first day, which turned out to be essential, having now drank the lot. Rosthwaite was the village where most were destined to stay that night but we had to take a detour to the nearby village of Stonethwaite arriving, very wearily, at Stonethwaite Farm. As its name suggests this was, I imagine, a typical Cumbrian working farm, the house being hundreds of years old, consequently the first thing you should take note of are the low ceiling. When I regained consciousness I made a mental note to walk around constantly looking upwards, for low beams in the ceiling, to avoid a repeat of the incident. Our bags had arrived, the accommodation was fine and as we had a sink in the room sharing the bathroom with other guests would not be a problem. First things first, the kettle went on then my sweaty clothing went in the sink, we had a small packet of washing powder just for this job, I used the shower, which worked fine, changed into clean clothes of course, then rested on the bed.

Taking a shower had a downside, the plaster on my foot had come off, although I'd now got fabricating them down to a fine art, but at this rate in three or four days I calculated I would run out of plasters and started to think what village on route would have, of all things, a plaster shop. Having re plastered my left foot we took a very gentle stroll down the village lane looking for the pub, checking a few times for reception on the mobile phone with negative results, soon coming up to the plush looking and lavishly named Langstrath Country Inn, which was absolutely packed out. This, without a doubt, must obviously be the pub Jack was talking about but, oh dear I thought, it's so popular you'll need to book a week in advance if you want to eat here and by now we were famished. Unlike the atmosphere in which we endured fried chicken and chips at the end of day one I'd been plunged into a smell of fine cuisine surrounded by food which looked absolutely exquisite, to add insult to injury a waitress wafted a mouth watering plate of stake and kidney pie right past my nose. I was in no way up for another walk to find somewhere else so as I ordered a pint of local ale, and a half pint for the wife of course, from a mature lady behind the bar then asked her firmly "what do we have to do to eat here?" She paused for thought while she took a good look at us then excused herself and disappeared through a door into the kitchen. I looked at Deborah about to ask what flavour crisps she'd like when the lady came back and said "there is a table in the restaurant available right now if you'd like it but we need it cleared again in an hour". "Perfect" I said, as she showed us to our table we grinned at each other with delight, and to top it off she promptly presented the menu which included my favourite gastronomic dishes. As if they knew what we were going to order the food arrived within minutes and, by the previous day's standard, was absolutely fantastic and beyond our expectations, just deserts for our long walk. Obliging the next diners with the table in good time we took our drinks into the pleasant floral smelling beer garden to do some people watching.

An hour or more passed as we relaxed outside in the beer garden, during which time we saw many people we were now acquainted with come and go. It wasn't necessary to converse, just raising a hand as a sign of recognition, was sufficient to acknowledge that we'd all achieved something today, a first for some, and for some an exceptional achievement. We asked around if anyone knew whether Peter and Brenda had eventually arrived safely and I was pleased, and I confess surprised, to hear someone say they had seen them.

It had been a hard day full of surprises with a twist of fate, how desperate must we have looked when asking for food? I was thankful that lady had not judged me on appearance, after all I was reasonably well dressed and too overweight to look poor. No, she'd paused to look much deeper and was then able to discern the difference between the look of appearance and my genuine emotional expression, sometimes we all have needs.

Chapter 3

I woke to complete silence, having had another good night's sleep, despite having the window open and expecting various farm yard noises I laid there, ears at maximum sensitivity, expecting at the very least to hear a bird twitter but there was absolutely nothing. The view from the window was limited by the towering fells so, from what I could see, my weather forecast was a positive bright and breezy day ahead. My foot was feeling fine, I decided not to bother with a shower, so get ready and resigned myself to making tea. Mindful not to bang my head we went in search of the dining room, after negotiating several flights of stairs we found a snug little basement farmhouse dining room waiting for us, tables all prepared, there was no one around so we sat down.

An age passed and I was beginning to wonder if we were actually in the right room when two elderly ladies joined us, chatting about something and everything one might expect two elderly ladies to be chatting about. Marg and Dot were jolly little souls and very upbeat about the day ahead, judging by her accent I'd say Dot was definitely from Scotland, yes, this time I'm sure I've placed her correctly. To me they looked very fit and lively, I was expecting them to be talking about the walk, but they seemed more excited about the food, saying they'd just seen the farmers wife collect the eggs that we were about to have for breakfast, I thought I'd better choose eggs. Much to my surprise, the two Australian ladies we met yesterday, Liz and Helen, also arrived for breakfast. They didn't tell me they were staying here, I thought, it hadn't cropped up in conversation yesterday, or if it had, I hadn't realised they were actually staying right here in this place. My wife says I don't pay attention which could be an explanation. It didn't particularly matter, I just thought it would have been good to know, sharing things with each other is good is it not? Perhaps I felt it might have helped me more than them. Suddenly I then realised I was the only bloke in the place and recalled the dreadful smell I'd left in the bathroom earlier, concluding everyone else would naturally assume it had to be me and that's what they'd all be thinking. Spontaneously, starting to feel embarrassed, I blurted out what a lovely day it was and asked everyone what their plans were for the day ahead, as a diversionary tactic, without really listening to their response.

During the silence, while I waited for my poached eggs on toast, Deborah motioned towards the visitors' book which had been left open on the next table and smiled. The last entry read "thanks for drying me out", a stark reminder what the weather is usually like here. I thought it worth pursuing this topic a little further and asked the Farmers wife, whilst she was serving my eggs, what the weather forecast was. "Oh you'll have a fine day today, good for walking" coming from a farmers wife I thought that was good news, "then rain on Tuesday", she said with a smirk and a strange little giggle as she left, bringing that conversation to an abrupt end. I couldn't think of anything I wanted to add to the visitors' book. Breakfast could not be faulted, fully satisfied with the excellent free range eggs, I departed gracefully being careful not to bang my head and returned to our room to carry out the departure procedure, choosing to wear the most comfortable socks I had, lacing up my boots and, lastly, waving our bags a fond farewell as we dropped them on the door step leaving Stonethwaite Farm behind.

Walking with my Map unfolded and held out at arms length I was pleasantly surprised to discover a little footbridge crossing the river, which meant we didn't have to retrace our steps too far before we were back on the right path. As we approached the bridge I could see all our dining companions already on the other side of the river, striding off into the distance, I thought our departure procedure must have caused the delay needed some fine tuning. It was confirmation we were going in the right direction and also they already know about the footbridge and hadn't shared that information with us either, so I put the map away. We hadn't walked far when I noticed Jacks' tall companion rapidly gaining on us, we'd met him in the pub last night, he was accompanied by two young ladies I'd never see before but there was no sign of Jack. I could hear voices as they were getting nearer so I turned round to say hello to see one of them leap over a convenient dry stone wall, squatting for a pee as she touched down, taking it in his stride he smiled and explained they'd persuaded Jack to take the bus because he wouldn't manage the hills today and that he'd met these two ladies who agreed to team up with him and they were planning to go all the way to Patterdale by the high route. On conclusion of his explanation the young lass jumped back over the wall and without a word walked on, "have a good day" I said. "We'll never see them again" I said to Deborah, "at their pace they'll be several days ahead of us when they finish".

Today they were going twice the distance of anyone else we now knew and they'd also chosen to walk over a few mountains on route, just to take in the scenery. What's more, the distance from A to B, in this terrain, doesn't relate to the time it takes. On a map we were only walking half the distance we walked yesterday, but it would take the same time to get there, so I tried to imaging the map in three dimensions and mentally prepare for some hill climbing. Deborah and I had discussed the alternative "high" route earlier but I successfully argued that resting my blistered foot as much as possible was best, there were plenty of days walking ahead of us. As I was thinking about all that we'd been happily following the path by the river and had now come to a dark rocky ravine. I could hear the river as picturesque waterfalls fell down the aptly named Eagle Crag which we now had to ascend. I looked up to see some distant figures to realise it was Jacks companion, together with his two ladies, climbing effortlessly. I thought now would also be a good time, before climbing Eagle Crag, to loose weight and find a place to deal with the call of nature. This slight pause was sufficient for us to see David and Caroline approaching so we deliberately walked a bit slower, pretending to study the map as if planning our ascent, to allow them to catch up. I honestly think they were genuinely pleased to see us. They too were going to Grasmere but would be staying there two nights because their hotel would only accept bookings for the whole weekend, however, because of our two shorter days and their one long day, of some 25 miles, this meant we would see them again and rendezvous in 4 days time at Kirkby Stephen.

Our conversation finally began to focus on today's route and they too had also chosen not to take the "high" route but keep to the, shall we say more manageable, lower route. After all the chit chat our immediate way ahead presented itself, up Eagle Crag, and demanded that a serious climb was in order so I decided the time had come to get on with it. After 20 minutes or so Dave and Caroline were several hundred yards below us but I was on a roll and heading for the summit intent on keeping going, the pain from my blister had suddenly relented accompanied with a damp feeling, suggesting it had burst, I became determined not to stop, becoming surprised with myself what the application of will power can really do. A blister in the scheme of things was insignificant the main event is the journey. How often do we let little things niggle us and allow them become our main focus, sometimes we moan about them all day, to the detriment of not seeing, or participating, in the bigger picture.

Sound was being carried by the wind which was rising up the rock face and, despite a distance of several hundred yards, I could clearly hear the conversation between Dave and Caroline which was becoming more and more exacerbated, ending with "I thought we were doing the low route" followed by a louder "I think you'll find that this is the low route dear!" which made me chuckle and, strangely, provided more energy to keep me going. At the summit the weather was still kind but there was a very cold wind. I was so hot from the climb I sat down to cool off, immediately removing boot and sock to examine my sore foot. I'd raced myself up the hill and had time to stick on a new plaster and put on clean dry socks before Deborah arrived, extremely out of breath I may add, we then had time to eat an apple before Dave and Caroline arrived. We were pleased with out performance and I felt good.

The summit was a cross roads of many footpaths and while we all sat there a father and son team appeared. They were on a different journey but were eager and excited to converse with some "Coasters" about walking, especially in the Lake District. Their personal goal was a low level walk around the lakes, rather than taking to the hills, and I suspect a male bonding expedition before the son, just about to start university, flies the nest, I checked he was also taking time to introduce his son to some fine real ale.

It was a welcome break but now I could sense my body temperature beginning to drop and noticed the wind was beginning to pick up by the speed at which low clouds were now flying just over our heads, from my experience at sea I'd say force 8. The clouds started getting lower, I was becoming concerned about visibility when suddenly, it was too late, we were engulfed in cloud and could see nothing. It was time to say a quick good bye, good luck, and set off, David and Caroline went ahead in search of the next wayside marker while I gave some careful thought about the potential gravity of our situation, deciding to loose altitude as soon as possible would be best. The guide book reference, believe it or not, is an old boot on a stick planted in a cairn in the middle of a peat bog, which we need to cross before starting our decent to Grasmere. As bizarre as it seemed it became essential to locate the boot on the stick to ensure we were heading in the right direction. This was the first time I'd experienced being in the middle of nowhere, unable to see any distinguishing landmarks or discernible paths, just acres and more acres of peat bog. I began to think it most unlikely we'd find a boot on a stick, needle in a haystack was more probable in this fog, I thought some bugger has bound to have moved it since the guide book was written. I started to consider alternatives to our dilemma like getting my compass out, let's face it, who on Earth in their right mind would wander around acres of peat bog all day looking for an old boot? After ten minutes we decided to spread out only to encounter Marg and Dot who were in exactly the same situation and had been wondering about searching for ages. We joined forces to see if the power of team work would help and, eventually, in a surprised and comical voice, David exclaimed he'd found the boot. No one was more amazed than me as we all headed towards his voice, in the thick fog, to find it was exactly as the Guide Book described it to be. The team work paid off and, very relieved, we all cheerfully set off together knowing we were heading in the right direction taking the sensible route, a gradual decent to Grasmere. A slight deviation to our left would have taken up onto the "High" route which would entail a long walk along the ridge in fog, something we were attempting to avoid at all costs.

As we descended out of the cloud we were presented with one of the most magnificent views I've seen of the Lakes and to our left the awesome jagged ridge, the "High" route, was now visible. Further on down the hill wonderful waterfalls appeared, as if by magic and strange rock formations that deserved a closer look. There is only one way to see this beauty, you can't get here by car, you have to walk, not only walk but struggle, sweat, bring food and water because it's going to take you some time and you'll have to pee behind a bush. This is the closest I can get to being in harmony with our planet even close to creation itself. The pretty meandering route down to Grasmere allowed David and Caroline to go at their pace, Dot and Marg at theirs and we are ours, which allowed us all to experience the peace and tranquillity surrounding us in our own way.

The town of Grasmere was gradually getting larger and, thinking that all the hard work was over, we slowed our pace right down to appreciate the natural beauty of this place in all its fullness. An hour or so later I was very surprised to discover two people we knew, the Australian ladies Liz and Helen, sat prominently on a huge boulder looking like they'd climbed Everest, eating their sandwiches, for me that said it all. As we strolled by a friendly hand gesture and smiles from ear to ear was sufficient to communicate what we were all thinking. Late afternoon came all too soon and we waited for David and Caroline to arrive to say good bye, hopefully it would be au revoir, since they were staying in Grasmere for two days. We walked together discussing our journey to date, and the many new experiences we'd had although we'd only met the other day. My mind wondered off and I tried applying some physics to explain how our meeting and parting with other walkers was like the ebb and flow motion of the tide, sooner or later we tended to pass by someone we'd already met, sometimes they were in front, sometimes behind. It was all a bit strange and, consequently, getting to know a bit more about each other each time it happens.

Then, startled by a noise from above, the chap we'd had breakfast with the day before descended upon us down a steep bank out of the trees. It turned out we were at the point where the "High" route and the "Low" route converge and, by coincidence if you believe in them, we'd all arrived there at exactly the same time. We all recognised one another of course but hadn't previously been introduced or engaged in any conversation. Chris introduced himself with a bubbly "hello"! Having been brave enough to take the high route, had said he'd been on his own all day without seeing anyone. Unless he didn't want to admit he'd got lost in the fog we were talking experienced walker and I couldn't see any point in debating our abilities so we walked for a while talking about where we lived. He turned out to be quite an amiable chap and we would no doubt meet him again as he was staying at the same pub as ourselves in Patterdale, should we get there.

If you didn't know, the poet William Wordsworth *I wondered lonely as a cloud* . . . . lived in Grasmere and it so happened we were walking through the very gardens near where he lived that apparently inspired some of his poems, Chris told me that. As we left the poet's garden we came to the road, Chris, David and Caroline turned right heading for their B&B's and we had to turn left so we parted company. By now my left foot was giving me jip enough to cause me to limp, thinking we were nearly there, my thoughts turned to a hot bath as we stopped to rummage through the rucksack for the precise address of the B&B, Town Head Farm, Grasmere was what we'd read the previous night but we'd missed out part of the address: Mill Bridge! This was not good news as Mill Bridge was two miles north and up hill from our current position, trying not to become annoyed we had little choice but to cheerfully march on.

Arriving at Town Head Farm, much wearier than anticipated, having gone the extra miles I saw a bench in the front garden and immediately sat down to remove my boots and give my sore foot some air. I was there a good five minutes before the lady of the house rushed up the path, straight past me, and into the house, then a minute later rushed out again with a friendly greeting, a cup of tea and a biscuit, having presumed correctly who we were. She spelled out the house rules, bathrooms, breakfast etc, then rushed off again. I couldn't work out if she was trying to run both the B&B and Farm on her own, which would be very demanding, or she was having a crisis. She leapt into her car, an old family four door that looked like it had never been washed, and was also home to half a dozen chickens and drove off not even bothering with her seat belt. I was hoping to embrace the slower peaceful way of life I expected to find in these remote country parts so we stayed in the garden to enjoy our cup of tea, simply enjoying the view as the day turned to evening, and we were still there when she returned home brandishing two strange looking hats, giving us a brief explanation of their history before planting them upon our heads and left. Despite a lengthy interrogation of the wife afterwards I was left very perplexed and never did understand what the Dickens she'd been talking about. On closer examination it could be said they resembled something Robin Hood might wear with a large Bumble Bee embroidered on the rim. The gist of the story was they had been hand made for two previous coasters, why and what happened to them still remained a mystery, but it had now, apparently, become our mission to wear them all the way to Robin Hoods Bay. It just seemed an appropriate time to nod and accept the situation so Deborah duly took a photo of me in the garden wearing the hat.

Food was going to be a requirement sooner rather than later so, looking at the map, the nearest pint of beer symbol suggested dinner might be just half a mile away on the main road toward Grasmere which I confirmed with the landlady on her return, it was called the Travellers Rest, she'd heard good reports, exactly what I needed. She went on to explain she'd received a phone call from the other couple who would be staying there that night to say they had taken a bus to the next town, as his wife was a Catholic and wanted to go to Mass that evening, so they would not be arriving 'till late. Too much information for me I thought, until I realised that they would be sharing the bathroom so perhaps now would be a good time to use it and leave the window open. Observing the ceiling height I took our bags to find our bedroom, the shower did its job and, as if it were by now second nature, we did our laundry in the sink. Realising that the radiators were not on, or likely to, we improvised a clothes hanger by fixing Deborah's extendable walking stick across the open window.

I manufactured yet another plaster to fit my left foot but this time it didn't take away the discomfort and I was beginning to wonder how much further I would be able to walk on it. I lay on the bed pondering my predicament until my stomach won the battle so down stairs I went and on went the boots, ouch. I stepped outside, grimacing as I put weight on my foot, map in one hand to ensure we took the most direct route rather than trusting my nose, and walking stick in the other. Deborah was searching for her walking stick and after too many minutes, becoming annoyed, I concluded that since it wasn't by the front door she must have left it when we stopped to say good bye to Chris, David and Caroline. There was no choice but to go back and look to see if was still there, the lost walking stick had suddenly gone to the top of the priority list as it was a present from her mum and dad. We'd only gone a few yards when the old four door chicken cope on wheels pulled up driven by our host, she said I'm going in your direction would you like a lift? How could we refuse? Brushing straw and chicken poo off the back seat we jumped in and, wanting to appear conversant with local customs, ignored the seat belt, partly out of choice and partly because it was trapped behind the back seat.

I thought she'd taken pity on me as her first question was about my limp and did I think it was going to be alright, then moving on to tell me about all the people who'd stayed at her B&B with exactly the same problem and how far they managed to get after they limped off the next morning. Thanks very much, I thought. I was grateful for the lift, at least it reduced the distance we had to walk back to where we thought we might find Deborah's walking stick, which sadly turned out to be in vain. Oh well, there wasn't much we could do or say about it, I was not fed up so I suggested we make a bee line to the pub across some farmers fields not bothering with any footpaths.

The Travellers Inn turned out to be a delightful old coaching house, the local beer and the menu looked tempting and the happy faces of the other customers who were eating invited us to stay. I have to say had it looked horrible we would have still eaten there anyway rather than walk elsewhere. Over a relaxing dinner we discussed the whereabouts of the lost walking stick and a multitude of possible solutions to the blister on my left foot, along with the possible routes for tomorrow's journey to Patterdale. Despite several pints of the landlords best brewed anaesthetic I took a very slow stroll back to the B&B to rest my foot as much as possible, arriving in the dark. The landlady was there to greet us and she offered us seats in the TV room and a nightcap, we thanked her but declined, the thought of looking at the TV was furthest from my mind. She said the other couple had phoned again saying they had missed the bus and were waiting for a taxi so she wasn't expecting them 'till 11.00pm. We indicated to our host what time we'd like breakfast and retired for the evening.

Strange, I thought, why people go to such lengths to attend worship. She must have felt a great need to go but why? Are we really called to conform so strictly to ritual or be free and get out there to meet others who have a greater need than our own? Perhaps we allow our daily lives to become a ritual, filled with excuses, that actively prevents us from finding time to interact with others as we should.

Chapter 4

I was just nodding off when I heard the sound of someone using the bathroom, the other couple must have arrived I thought. Despite being disturbed at such a crucial moment I couldn't help being amused and found myself struggling not to giggle out loud. The sounds I could hear brought back visions of my earlier experience when I made a similar muffled arghhh, accompanied by a lively dance, whilst stark naked trying to adjust the temperature of the shower, eventually figuring out the hot and cold taps were labelled incorrectly.

I was woken by rays of bright sunshine streaming in through our little cottage bedroom window, just above my socks, synchronising my body clock like pressing the reset button on a stopwatch. I gave it a moments thought but there was no possibility of a "lie in" so I leapt out of bed to test my left foot, which felt surprisingly good, to promptly put the kettle on. I made my wife a cup of tea, as one would on such a beautiful morning then, remembering that the hot and cold tap were reversed, I took a long hot shower and sat on the bed to manufacture another dressing for my foot. The weather looked good enough to consider whether or not to put on my zip off trousers that could convert to shorts and also good enough to consider attempting Striding Edge and, of course, free range eggs on toast. What a joy in life to be only concerned about such things! I looked at Deborah as she was feeling our socks that were hanging up, to see if they were dry, and by the expression on her face they were still damp. Realising they were hanging on her walking stick I simply stared at her until the penny dropped, mystery of the lost walking stick solved!

The Farmhouse dining room was inviting, panelled in old oak from floor to ceiling with a bare oval oak breakfast table sat in the middle set for four, the total sum of guests. The room exuded an aura of timeless and relaxing scent of furniture wax. We were first to arrive immediately followed by our landlady who must have heard us and, in a chirpy mood asked what we would like to eat, then looked at me with a surprised expression, presumably because we didn't order her full English breakfast which she so eloquently described. For all I know we could have missed out on the best bacon this side of Swindon, she left us alone and went off into the kitchen to prepare eggs on toast and our packed lunches. After about ten minutes I could hear the other couple coming down the wooden stairs, there was a distinctive gap in their arrival and no explanation, suggesting to me they'd had a slight quarrel. Robin introduced himself and immediately started to explain what had happened the previous evening, reinforcing my thought that they'd had a tiff. He said his wife was a Catholic, implying that he was most definitely not and that was the cause of all their problems, being Saturday she wanted to attend Mass so they had to catch a bus to a suitable Church which turned out to be miles away in the next town. They decided to find somewhere to eat and then missed the last bus back, didn't have any cash, didn't know what to do next, and on and on he went until Tricia, his wife, started her defence. This opened up an interesting conversation and suddenly Robin was on his back foot, he confessed he wasn't a Christian, just attended church to please his wife and manoeuvred the conversation to the journey. Breakfast arrived and the conversation about the walk continued, he produced a diary which he'd written four years ago then went on to read from it and tell us how long each stage of the journey had taken them. He'd painstakingly recorded each detail of the journey and the time of each section to the minute. Since Tricia's knee was giving her trouble they emphasised that they would be walking at a leisurely pace, I wasn't trying to think of an excuse to say I'd prefer not to walk with them, but I was pleased to hear that which saved me the bother. Returning to the subject of Tricia's knee Deborah said we would pray for her, specifically healing for her knee, which she welcomed so we did. Robin was definitely taken aback and the prayer brought breakfast to a resounding conclusion. We rose from the table with an amicable farewell realising it was very likely we would meet again, somewhere along our journey.

Fed and watered it was time to depart, after using the bathroom and packing the bags of course, leaving the bags where they were found for the Sherpa van to transport them to our next lodgings, another routine which was becoming second nature. Stuffing our packed lunches into our rucksacks, collected from the lady in the kitchen, we said goodbye, checking with each other we had our walking sticks as we did so. Just outside the doorway I halted to lace up my boots good and tight before striding off into the distance, resisting the urge to look back, preferring to press on and conquer any hills that lay ahead.

There were so many possible routes today we were spoilt for choice, the first obstacle was called the "Tongue". As I gazed up I could see this was an apt name for this great long hill rising out of Grasmere with a valley down the middle outlined with a path to the left and to the right, both paths meet at either end so choosing which one didn't really seem to matter. Secondly the options, should we get there, were between Striding Edge, St. Sunday Crag, or an easy path straight down the middle, whatever we decide, either route would lead us to Patterdale and the good news was that weather was on our side.

The first choice was taken in a slightly flippant manner, similar to tossing a coin, resulting in us choosing the left option up the Tongue, not that I could see it mattered, however it turned out we were alone and I was therefore pleased, the only other walkers we could see were miles away on the right hand path. As we began our ascent it wasn't long before I soon began to huff and puff but I was feeling fit, having kept the number of beers to a minimum last night, and even started to think that today we could attempt Striding Edge.

We made good progress up the Tongue, my foot wasn't troubling me as much as I expected, turning around just occasionally to admire the view of Grasmere in the distance seeing it get gradually smaller and smaller. As the left and right hand routes started to converge we looked across at the other walkers trying to identify who they might be but the distance was too great and we didn't have binoculars, we arrived at the point at which the two paths converged expecting to see people about but there was no one in sight. The path began to level off but despite the fact that we had been climbing all morning we still found ourselves surrounded by hills. I was completely taken by surprise to find we'd come to a lake, called a Tarn, about a hundred yards across, nestled in a dip, and appearing like a mirror.

The path descended gradually, a welcome relief for my muscles, leading to the edge of the Tarn which invited us to stop and rest a while to enjoy this beautiful place.

Whenever we stop we always seem to have a bite to eat and this time was no exception, but I thought we deserved it after the brisk climb up the Tongue. It was also time to study the map and deliberate our next route. We had stopped by Grisedale Tarn, to our left rose Dollywagon Pike, the way up to Helvellyn and Striding Edge, and to our right lay the option of St Sunday Crag. Alternatively, if we didn't fancy any mountain climbing, there was a simple walk straight down the middle. I verbally delivered the options to Deborah, casually munching on a banana trying to make out it would be no big deal, asking if she felt like attempting Striding Edge or St Sunday Crag and left her to think on it. After some consideration, the weather being in our favour and feeling up to the challenge, I said I was up for Striding Edge and finally Striding Edge won.

As we set off again to make our way to the base of Dollywagon Pike and start our ascent we could see Marg and Dot sat having lunch so went over to say hello. It turned out to be quite a lengthy and interesting discussion. They were clearly enjoying their journey and were happy to share their news with us, doing the walk to raise funds for charity, their itinerary was similar to ours for most of the route so, likely as not, we would be seeing them again in the days ahead. We discussed the options immediately ahead but they were clearly against attempting Striding Edge favouring the easy way down and presenting a convincing argument to support their decision.

Unperturbed by Marg and Dots' argument we eagerly set off for Striding Edge. It was a truly steep climb up Dollywagon Pike, not many words were said until I suddenly blurted out "good morning", looking up to catch a glimpse of a young fell runner come haring down past me. I stopped and turned to look in amazement, and with a feeling of admiration, to see the young chap disappearing out of sight. Before I could think of something else to say two mountain bikers did the same, this was obviously a hill that some people with a certain disposition saw as a challenge. It reminded me of the time I met a fell runner in a pub in York just a few weeks earlier. It was just one of those occasions where we'd had a few beers and somehow got talking, I recall him, with amusement, making the blindingly obvious statement "you can be absolutely knackered running up hill for half an hour"!

I arrived at the top of Dollywagon Pike some way nearer to understanding the mindset of a fell runner, Deborah and I paused for a while to admire the view. The long flat walk to the summit of Helvellyn became tiring, the wind was picking up and we had to stop a couple of times, the second time to put on waterproofs as the temperature had noticeably dropped. I identified the summit as a spot where a multitude of brightly clothed people had gathered. I concluded they must be weekenders who had decided on a challenging days walk since they were trying to stand in the strong wind for absolutely no reason I could think of, other than they'd got there. Without hesitation we headed off to the right as soon as possible to get down out of the wind and to look down on Striding Edge.

Music: Variations on an Original Theme Opus 36, Enigma, by Edward Elgar

If there has to be one picture in this book it is this one taken of Striding Edge and Red Tarn, you can just make six chaps dressed as Father Christmas coming up, they were singing carols.

As you can see from the photo, we didn't need to refer to the map, the route along the ridge being obvious even to a novice on such a clear day. I can appreciate that some might take issue with the definition of "walking" here, as it requires hands as well as feet in order to cling on, even without the gale force wind. There was no going back now so, knowing Father Christmas had done it, we confidently set off soon realising we were the only ones going down and everyone else was coming up, consequently we therefore had to wait patiently in several places where the path narrowed to a knife-edge allowing only one person at a time to pass. An hour later we looked back and were feeling rather pleased with ourselves, our faces no doubt expressing a sense of accomplishment to those we passed coming up as I greeted each one with a hearty "good afternoon"!

The hard work completed we were left with just a few miles left to walk, down hill all the way to Patterdale, just a joyful afternoons stroll. To confirm it I looked at the map and sure enough it didn't look much further, I was grateful it wasn't another long day as my sore foot was beginning to complain along with my quadriceps after that steep decent. As time went on my blister was starting to complain more and more with each step and although we'd had a great day I was hoping we'd soon arrive, for some reason I couldn't help thinking about tomorrow. Our journey the next day, from Patterdale to Shap, was going to be our longest and most arduous day and I had to confront my main two adversaries; my foot and the weather.

As we arrived in Patterdale I stepped onto the pavement, thinking level ground would help, a pavement was something I hadn't walked on for days but it didn't do as I expected and relieve the pain. Our B&B was also the only pub in Patterdale and although it was less than a mile to go I was now resenting each step I was obliged to take. To compound the issue the village was full of walkers witnessing my arrival. By now it looked like many of them were heading for their cars to go home, for a Sunday afternoon it was like being among Monday morning commuters. To my delight I recognised a couple of faces, Marg and Dot came walking towards us, and out of politeness and curiosity we stopped to talk. They weren't staying in the pub but had walked to it, and back again through the village looking for their lodgings to no avail. I decided to help and got out a local map, thankful for a moments rest. It was no failing on their part, Rose Cottage, Patterdale, was the address they were looking for. It wasn't on my map either and, out of the few houses in the village. I also pictured it would be one that looked like a cottage with a rose climbing up it. Unable to assist, concluding it must be tucked away down some remote farm track, they said cheerfully "that looks like a B&B sign at the end of that lane up there, we'll go in that direction" so we said "good bye see you tomorrow" and off they went still cheerful.

As we turned the next corner I thought I could see the pub, there were dozens of happy people sat drinking in the garden but as we approached I was dismayed to find it was actually a hotel, not our pub, rather than pass by I confess I was tempted to book in. There was only one pub in Patterdale and for some bizarre reason unknown to me someone had decided not to do the sensible thing and build it by the church where you would expect to find it. No, someone in the past had decided to make my live difficult right now and I would like to have a word with them. For some reason I was reminded of the sentiments expressed by the lady in our last B&B which gave me the determination to hobble on. I can't express the relief when we turned the next corner to see the sign, White Lion Inn.

Music: Vivaldi, Gloria in Excelcis Deo!

It was now early evening and the pub was so busy we had to fight our way in, which in my book is a generally good sign, or had they got a captive audience I began to wonder, being the only watering hole for miles around. No, it looked like a good old fashioned pub serving good honest food and good beer, I felt so relieved knowing that we wouldn't have to walk anymore today.

I left my boots on and fought my way to the bar, which felt like today's main objective, although tempted by a beer right there and then I just wanted the room key. This time, to prevent them walking, two keys came attached to logs the size you'd happily throw on the fire at Christmas. Our bags were found with some others in a heap suggesting there were other Coasters still to arrive. This was a pub with welcome written all over it, I found out there was no need to remove our walking boots, which was a good thing as the landlord himself was showing us the way up to our room and I was still wearing mine. The doors in the old pub were awkward enough and the stairs were narrow to say the least, negotiating them carrying anything more than a newspaper was quite impossible consequently every visitor's bag had torn its own shaped groove in the wallpaper. That'd keep a forensic scientist happy I thought if one should ever walk here. Every light had to be turned on so we could see our way and the old pub charm was becoming lost in last century's attempt at modernisation.

The door to our room swung opened with a loud creak, it was a tight squeeze but Deborah and I managed to get in with the bags, thankfully we hadn't brought the dogs but I suspect they would have been more than welcome were there room. I noticed the landlord was still waiting outside so I looked at him as if he was expecting a tip, thankfully not, he was dangling a key waiting to deliver the next surprise. Without a word we followed him twenty foot down the corridor to the bathroom that was the door the other key was for. He kept emphasising that it was our bathroom solely for our use, no one else could use it, it's just for us. He even operated all the lights and taps and only when he'd convinced himself we understood the situation he left. In all the excitement I'd forgotten to ask whether we needed to book a table for dinner. All things considered I thought our compact little room would more than suffice the window looked out onto the vast hillside rather then the road so we should be in for a quite night's sleep and our washing should by dry in the morning. Deborah was already emptying the bags, intent on taking a shower. I decided to take my boots off before lying on the bed and not bring up the subject about eating that evening, satisfied there would be no problem when it came to being fed.

Having our own little bathroom turned out to be a real blessing and we soon turned it into a full scale laundrette, a great result, it even had a large electric heated towel rail, perfect! Virtually everything we had went through the wash and hung on the towel rail to dry ready for tomorrow's long haul, there'd be no shortage of clean dry socks. My turn for the shower came and at the moment when I was completely covered in soap, without any warning, the water temperature immediately turned freezing cold, so cold I could hardly get my breath. I frantically started twiddling all the knobs but within less than ten seconds I gave up and leapt out, the water out of all the taps was the same, blimey what an experience. Cold wet and shivering I returned to the bedroom to tell Deborah my plight, she laughed so I did too, at least I'd stopped thinking about my blister. I recalled having a similar experience on a camp site some forty years earlier when the shilling in the electric meter ran out. I took a moment to rest in the peace and quiet with the window open, reflecting on the day, soothed by the unspoilt view, no doubt shared by many over thousands of years, before limping down to the bar for something to eat.

The place was absolutely packed out and I had to shout at the barmaid to be heard, something I detest having to do. Consoled by the locally brewed beers on offer and the availability of homemade food, which was a real blessing, we just needed to find a table to sit down at. I started to scan each table in turn in the vain hope of finding an empty pudding bowl, indicating someone was about to vacate a table, but it looked hopeless. I was just working on plan B when my eye caught someone waving frantically from the far distant corner, it was Brenda and Peter, they'd obviously realised our predicament and were beckoning us over. Raising my eyebrows with great surprise and genuine gladness, in acknowledgement, I nudged Deborah and we fought our way over, expressing our thanks we managed to perch on a couple of old milking stools at the end of their table feeling, there was room for a dinner plate so it felt snug and cosy, I was installed for the evening.

It's not very often we meet people from Canada so I presumed there would be much to discuss and there was. I'd been to Vancouver and skiing in Whistler once so I could always pitch that into the conversation should we run out of words. It turned out that Peter was a director of a financial business, that had done really well, and he'd just sold it and taken early retirement to live by a lake in British Columbia. The obvious question came to mind so I asked why come here to do the Coast to Coast walk? Peter remained silent and pointed his finger at Brenda who said she had read about it in a book and, whilst they were over here visiting some long lost relatives, thought it would be a good idea, Peter then added all the details including how unprepared they were for this walk and today they'd seen the air ambulance bring in a wounded walker from Striding Edge, additional third party information from the bar told us that someone was blown off last week, when it was a bit windy, to their death.

They said this journey was marketed as a walk in the Park, and thinking Britain was flat, which it probably is relative to the Rockies, they didn't think they would need things like walking boots, well that explained a lot! I presume they missed out "National" Park. Anyhow, the one thing that came out of the conversation was that there are no Sheep in Canada. That was certainly news to me so a jolly evening was had with good conversation, lubricated by fine beer, about the many breeds of sheep we'd passed en route and indeed eaten whilst waiting for Deborah's Herdwick Shank to arrive and my lamb curry. I was just about to go off the deep end when Deborah gently nudged me, indicating I'd lost count of the number of beers I'd had, and sensibly we concluded by agreeing to rendezvous for breakfast.

The bed had a soft deep mattress and was jammed against three walls, climbing in required a manoeuvre like getting into a hammock on a submarine, but once installed I was surprisingly comfortable. Thinking of the discussion over dinner I began to wonder if, as much as the Canadian couple were ill prepared practically, I was as ill prepared mentally. After that awakening analysis I realised I hadn't discussed the blister on my foot! Probably a good thing over dinner, but lying in bed I could now feel it throbbing so I starting to give it some serious thought, puzzling how to manage the problem for the best . . . . tomorrow we were walking to Shap! It was going to be a long day, twice the distance we had done today and up hill all the way, so my mind became focused on finding a solution. The Chocolate bars we'd accumulated so far on route would be good for energy, we should plan regular stops to take on water and food, the only other thing I needed for my left foot was comfort and a steady pace. I lay there awake as the hours ticked by until finally I'd got it, this sounds so simple, my conclusion was to wear two pairs of socks, actually that would be three layers as one pair would be the 1000 mile guaranteed no blisters socks with integral lining, no rubbing guaranteed. That would solve it I thought, double socks! I would now be able to get off to sleep without worrying, unfortunately it doesn't quite work like that so I started to wonder what to say about Striding Edge . . . . it can be a bit tricky, now and then there will be a broken limb or two, very occasionally someone will be blown off if it's a bit windy but I think it's worth the effort. Advice; be prepared physically and mentally.

Still awake I started to recall the earlier cold shower episode with much amusement when there was a laud baaaaaaaaaa from outside our window. The curtains were not drawn, the window was wide open and it was pitch black outside, a sheep must have bedded down for the night right outside the window, could I be bothered getting out of bed to do something about it? No. Half an hour later, after the fifteenth baaaaaaaaaa, I gave in and got out of bed to close the window, fumbling about in the complete darkness, trying not to make a noise myself and disturb the wife. I decided to visit the bathroom, and started the search for our private bathroom key, minutes later when I slowly opened the door it creaked enough to wake everyone in the place, it was just like door sounds in a horror film. The ten yard dash to the bathroom and back followed by the creaking door started to make me laugh, I returned to bed bemused by the day's events.

Chapter 5

I rolled out of bed and headed straight for the window poking my head out to see the reason for my disturbed nights sleep in the form of a ewe lying comfortably against the wall a couple of feet beneath our window. Although we were upstairs the Pub was cut into the hillside, which rose very steeply, so in our room we were effectively at ground level. The ewe was just lying there unperturbed, I was close enough to lean out and touch her, I couldn't help thinking that perhaps she would soon be on the menu. After a cup of tea the next item for consideration was the shower and whether or not to risk it another time. This old pub had many a tale to tell including that William Wordsworth was in the bar when news arrived that Nelson had died at Trafalgar, I bet he wasn't brave enough to take a shower here, so thinking of Nelson in I went and thankfully, on this occasion, the plumbing behaved itself. Back in the room careful attention was given to my blister, today's journey justified a new plaster, cut exactly to the right shape, then three layers of socks ensuring no wrinkles. The boots went on and all felt fine, that was the ticket, today was going to be a good day!

At the exact time breakfast was suppose to start we set foot in the dining room, in fact the same room we ate in last night, to find Peter and Brenda again, plus an Australian couple we hadn't previously met, and another couple who didn't look like they were about to set off walking at all. They were sat waiting at empty tables with a pile of bags in the middle of the floor, no doubt packed ready for transport to Shap. We struck up light hearted conversation which was more about where we'd all come from and what it was like back home rather than the day ahead, which, on a positive note was probably a good thing, anything to avoid starting the day already disillusioned. I thought Deborah and I were the ones who'd be first ready in the morning, and we hadn't even packed our bags yet. We were ready for breakfast to the minute they said they start serving and I couldn't help ponder if it was known to be such an arduous day that everyone else had started out before breakfast. That just didn't make sense and remained a mystery.

As much as the full English was tempting we knew we had a long walk ahead so it was time to stock up on carbohydrates in the form of more and more eggs on toast. It was becoming a bit of a smelly diet. Full of countless toasted slices of white bread I negotiated the stairs for the last time, bag in hand, Deborah bringing up the rear holding the sticks and room key which we exchanged for our packed lunches.

We were off to Shap, the fresh morning air lightening our steps as we headed down the high street, carefully looking for the first landmark that marked our route. Having gone less than a hundred yards there was Robin and Tricia coming out of a little shop on the opposite side of the street, which was so busy that it required investigating. The opening hours were unbelievably early, obviously they were supplying walkers with packed lunches and breakfast baps. I figured most of the troops had already left and got under way early so we'd better press on.

In no time at all we'd left Patterdale, turned left, and started to climb. The guide book said today we would have to climb 1300 metres, there are no places to stay and no shops for the next 16 miles, we were positive we had all that was required in our rucksacks so it was going to be a case of keeping mind, body and soul in harmony. As we could see the path stretching out before us we could also see more and more walkers. As we climbed I noticed the distance was growing between Robin and Tricia and between me and Deborah, I just said hello to Tricia as we passed knowing there would be an opportunity for conversation later in the day. Challenged by the hill it looked like everyone ahead was walking alone preferring to find their own pace and space to keep going. I concluded it was best not to stop and do the same and after a while I found my body adjusting to the environment, or my predicament, and going up hill strangely ceased to be a task and the reason for being there started to make sense. If you're looking for an obvious explanation you'll be disappointed, to be quite frank I don't have one you have to try this yourself, but as the path levelled off I was on the look out for a dry comfortable rock to sit on, along with everyone else, to admire the views and greet those behind me with a grin of success.

All collected and composed again we now had miles of peat bog ahead, and from my last experience I was expecting the path to disappear, however it was quite windy so not as boggy as expected. The four of us set off together soon finding Marg and Dot ahead, walking somewhat indecisively with a few some new faces we'd never seen before. They seemed pleased to see us and keen to chat, bringing everyone else into a general nondescript conversation which was very amicable but served to cement the party together. We were not climbing anymore, walking was leisurely, and after a couple of miles we collected some more Coasters and the group grew to a dozen. It was a diverse group of different ages, backgrounds, nationalities, all finding themselves walking on a peat bog together and all enjoying the moment. How bizarre.

I'm aware that a group can develop its own dynamics and this became evident when we started to climb what was thought to be "The Knot" but I was uncertain. I decided I must stop and consult the map, it was difficult to judge precisely where we were from the distant land marks but eventually I managed to convince them we were going up "Rest Dodd" and not "The Knot". After vaguely heading for the right path I was very relieved when the evidence was compelling and we were definitely back on the right route, even more relived to save an hour on our day.

Behind us I could hear what sounded like an army of Australians so I decided it was time to take evasive action and find my own space again. We sheltered out of the wind behind a dry stone wall, deciding to stop and eat, letting them pass by. The left foot blister was holding up well with the double sock solution, I took my boots off to give it some air but, so far, this was good news. Taking a rest, not wanting to eat too much, we watched everyone climb "The Knot" until they disappeared out of sight allowing us to be completely on our own again for our ascent.

As we were on our own it was doubly imperative to ensure we kept to the preferred route, there was a turn which someone said earlier is easy to miss, so, concerned about it I kept the map in my hand until folding it in the strong wind became such a farce I gave up. Finding the left turn was not so bad but as we started to climb up the ridge towards Kidsty Pike the wind picked up significantly and we looked at one another, probably thinking of the poor soul who was blown off Striding Edge. It was still a long way up to the top and although it wasn't raining we stopped to reach for our waterproofs, emotions dithering between fear and funny, as we wrestled to put the billowing garments on.

At 780 metres above sea level, the highest point on the route, I was being blown sideways and walking at 45 degrees. It was pointless trying to speak but I did want to say to Deborah I was glad we weren't crossing Striding Edge today. I can only equate the experience to the equivalent of sky diving for half an hour wearing a plastic Mac and shorts. We made the top of Kidsty Pike, and being the highest point on our journey, celebrated by stopping for a few seconds to admire the view before rapidly starting our decent, passing two young chaps on their way up, our facial expressions saying more than words.

It was soon apparent that one of the consequences of going up was coming down. I was grateful the wind was dying down in some sort of inverse exponential function, but the decent to Haweswater was steep to say the least. My knees were holding up surprisingly well as they resisted gravitational forces dragging me down the hill at a rate of knots, passing everyone we'd let pass us earlier, who'd all chosen to stop for lunch in the same spot, but after several miles of pounding I began to wonder what they would be like the next morning.

Music Libertango, by Astor Piazzolla

We decided to carry on right down to the lake shore before stopping for our lunch and a very welcome stop it was too. The guide book describes the day as involving some serious "long haul trekking" and as I studied the map it was clear the walk along the lake was going to take at least a couple of hours. I suddenly realised I changed to using time instead of distance and, calculating our arrival time, became more concerned that we needed to maintain a good pace to get there before it went dark. It had certainly been the most demanding day so far, but the good news was it wasn't raining and my blood sugars were not in danger of plummeting due to the stash of chocolate bars we'd stored up over the last four days. We enjoyed a feast while everyone walked passed us again.

Anyone could be forgiven for thinking that a walk along a lake would be quite flat, perhaps similar to walking along a sandy beech, but this was not to be the case. Any thoughts I'd had of an easy two hour stroll were soon dismissed, this section, true to the guide book, required some serious trekking.

After my estimated two hours the end of the lake was still nowhere in sight, my foot was hurting more than ever before and I was beginning to feel downhearted. In an attempt to lessen the pain and shorten time I tried short bursts of running but this had no effect, it was like closing your eyes when you don't want anyone to see you.

Persevering for endless miles with my, now painful, left foot we finally left the lake shore behind us skirting the edge of a village, or somewhere that resembled civilisation, to find Marg and Dot sat on a bench by a red phone box. They were staying in a B&B several miles away and were waiting for a lift. Whilst talking we also bumped into Chris, who would be staying on the other side of the lake that night, so he walked off on his own. Oh well, good for them, but our resting place was miles ahead so we pressed onward. Thankfully the path became easier under foot, following a river upstream, however, as we came to some woodland I had to take time out to sit on a convenient old fallen down Oak tree for a rest and to remove my boots and socks.

It then stuck home that time was not a problem, we would arrive when we arrive, this was the mistake I made on day one. I wasn't in a race, why had I concerned myself so much I wondered? While I was pondering on that to my surprise, nonchiently meandering through the woods, came Peter and Brenda. I wondered if they'd taken a different route, they didn't look windswept. A Canadian logger's cry of "Hello" was heard when Peter saw me. I gave a loud wave back as they carried on through the wood, I wondered for a moment why they didn't come over. I presumed they thought I'd stopped for a nature break and decided to politely continue on their way.

I studied the map again but whatever units I applied whether it be hours, minutes, miles or kilometres didn't make any difference, the bottom line was we still had a long way to go. One bonus was the lovely late summers evening by the river, ideal for a walk. A few miles later it was our turn to pass Brenda and Peter sitting on a fallen tree by the river, looking content but perhaps in need of a rest, so we simply gestured as we passed by, we hadn't seen anyone else now for miles so I figured we must be the stragglers.

Aiming next for Shap Abbey we became, a little slightly in the scheme of things, completely lost. We were attempting to cross a wide open field where there were no signs or visible paths so, giving up trying to find the path, we finally headed in a general direction towards the river. Eventually, to my surprise, what do I see? Brenda and Peter heading towards us, also lost. Finding ourselves in the same boat we collectively pulled our resources together and set search for a tiny footbridge across the river. This was just what we needed to lift our spirits, I'm sure our predicament came about due to weariness, although non of us would admit it, but at least we were working together with the same mutual objective; to get to Shap! Sharing the difficulties of the day and the task of finding the route in jovial conversation was, I have to say, a new experience for me. It raised the bar of what could be achieved to another level by sharing the problem without even consciously realising we needed to. I was worried this was starting to become natural, it felt good. Perhaps this was just a glimpse of the type of resourcefulness people had to get through the war. Although I wouldn't normally admit to it I needed help and I was grateful they came along at that time.

Arriving at Shap Abbey, as its name suggests, we came upon the old ruins of an Abbey. Stopping to indulge ourselves with a quick look then, feeling quite weary now, continued onward and upwards to Shap itself. All equally flagging, and desperate for encouraging words, the last mile we did on the road rather than the path across another muddy field, finally entering the North end of Shap.

Shap is, of course, famous of being the highest place on the old road to Glasgow the M6 motorway now bypasses the town bringing much less trade. We plodded down the old depressed high street trying to explain the history of where we were to Brenda and Peter and the significance of this old place. Words were drying up, Deborah was shattered bless her, and Brenda and Peter would not be stopped entering by the very first watering hole we came to. As we passed the first pub they headed straight in saying "are you coming for a beer?" I looked back towards Deborah who was 100 yards behind and without saying anymore they noted my situation and said "goodbye" and that was it, they were gone. I was too tired to realise that was probably the last time I would see them and I hope they were too. I tried to devote some energy to motivate Deborah "it couldn't be far now love" is all I could muster. Our hostelry was defiantly on the main road, the Greyhound Inn, normally that would make me think of our dogs but not this time, in fact it wouldn't have bothered me if it turned out to be a kennel for the night.

How long was this A6 I wondered? It was now dusk and there was no one around to ask, I thought I was doing my best to convince my wife, who was rightly moaning, we were headed in the right direction and so we carried on. Seizing the opportunity, under pressure from the doubting wife, I asked the first local chap we came across, who was probably just starting his night shift, "where's the Greyhound?" and to my dismay he replied about a mile on the left. At least we were going in the right direction but another mile was the last thing we wanted to hear.

Eleven hours had passed since we left the pub in Patterdale and we must have looked pretty dishevelled as we entered the four star Greyhound Inn at Shap but I didn't care, what a good result, four stars! I was so pleased for Deborah even she couldn't moan at the facilities. It passed all the criteria I had applied for good walking accommodation with merit; clean, hot water, kettle, heated towel rail, thick toilet paper, it must be thick enough to prevent your fingers going through, a towel big enough to dry yourself, good food and perhaps most important for me of course some good beer. It ticked every box and after a good shower to revive us we fell into the bar and ordered food from the a la carte menu, after a beer of course. Phew, we'd arrived.

A long haired scruffy looking guy at the bar looked over and started conversation, he'd seen us arrive, and sussed us out immediately. "Did you come over Kidsy Pike" in the wind today? He started, I nodded, trying to weigh him up, the conversation rapidly developed into detail about the walk. In summary it turns out he'd done this journey twenty four times, mostly as a guide for American Tourists who fly over to Britain just to do the walk. I was actually not interested in listening and more concerned with the food which thankfully arrived and stopped the conversation. I couldn't fault it, just another beer was needed over which we discuss how well we'd coped with the most demanding and longest day so far and how on Earth I'd managed it with my sore left foot. There would be no problem sleeping tonight. I was pleased we taken the soft option tomorrow and were stopping half way to Kirby Stephen at Orton, a mere 8 miles. Good night.

Chapter 6

If I'm ever near Shap in the future I'll probably stay at the Greyhound. For certain I'll reminisce about the last time I stayed, and probably bump into the guy at the bar, but the Hotels' other attributes are worth it alone, or to put it another way there wasn't much else in Shap. That morning I opened my eyes feeling surprisingly awake, hesitantly I slowly went though the process of getting put of bed into the full standing up position and to my surprise finding no ill effects of yesterdays long trek. As I stretched in all directions, I was almost disappointed to discover my back was still connecting top and bottom parts together as it should and very surprised no body parts complained as I reached for the kettle. More than that, the laundry was dry, the shower temperature infinitely controllable, and my wife was feeling equally surprised by our level of fitness, smiling comfortably as I woke her with a cup of tea. Clearly the months of preparation had all been worth it.

Today was going to be a relatively short stroll to Orton, not that I had the faintest idea where it was, and with a touch of sadness coupled with a sense of achievement, we were leaving our friends the Lakes and hills behind.

There was no rush, I thought, as we were last to arrive for a leisurely breakfast, more eggs on toast? I think not, the full English looked too tempting and bring on the Black Pudding, we were on holiday so surly with only 8 miles to do I could indulge myself?

Perusing the Map over a very substantial breakfast we decided not to dally too much so that we'd have some tourist time in Orton. The bags had to be downstairs in time to be collected by 8.30am so that became our "cue" to get under way.

The departure ritual was now down to a fine art: Water bottles topped up, feet in two socks, Packed Lunch collected as we dropped off the room key, walking stick in hand and off we jolly well go.

From our hotel the map indicated there was a footpath, across the fields behind where we were staying, which lead to a footbridge over the M6 motorway only a mile or so away. This would bring us right back on route so, rather than retrace our steps heading back into Shap, we decided to take a slight detour. The roar of the Manchester to Glasgow express train confirmed our position but we could see no footbridge or means of crossing the railway. Our bold start that morning had soon become a hesitant one, in fact after less than a mile, we were forced to stop and get the map out again. Thankfully before I became annoyed we came to a tiny pedestrian tunnel to pass under the main railway line, I was thinking that crossing the railway was sort of a milestone along our walk, but I bet not many had used that particular route through the tunnel which was built over 150 years ago.

Heading across several fields, climbing over barbed wire and a couple of fences which seemed to be in the wrong place, I explained to the wife we'd obviously strayed slightly but we were accurately following the footpath exactly as it appeared on the map, clearly the locals do not use a map and they've made a footpath around the back somewhere. Confident in my map reading skills, but more likely convinced by the increasing traffic noise, she followed, and sure enough we soon came to the path leading up to the bridge over the motorway.

Standing on the bridge to observe the motorway traffic tearing up and down, for me, was a moment to savour. Memories flooded back to all those times I'd travelled under this bridge from the first time dad drove me and mum to Scotland in an old Austin A35 van, the bonnet catch fell off somewhere around here and we even stopped to look but never found it, to all the whys, when's, wherefore's on my journeys. I wondered if the motorists were looking up at us thinking, where are they going?

The bridge provided a great vantage point to see if any walkers were either coming or going, after all it was the highest point around, but we couldn't see anyone in either direction. If Peter and Brenda were in front of us now then we were unlikely ever to see them again, I was convinced some must be behind us, Chris and the two ladies must be at least several hours behind. The other feature on the landscape our eyes were drawn to was the quarry, this was a place of some serious excavation over many a year. The weather? Well apart from a few clouds and a cool breeze it looked like we were in for another fine day, being a walk of only eight miles this was a day off!

Thoughts of motor cars were still in my head as our journey continued along the adverse camber of the motorway embankment for a while, climbing slightly before the path fell to cross a quarry road and into open fields until the traffic noise started to subside. This was the time I realised we had left the hills behind, the landscape began changing to open fields, with the occasional group of tall trees, no doubt deliberately planted ages ago, for some forgotten reason, sadly now serving as a feeble wind break and walkers toilet.

Leaving the motorway brought a return to peace and quiet which was very welcome but became occasionally shattered, by the roar of a jet fighter who's pilot was certainly giving it the beans and flying low enough to read our map. Today, for some reason, it wasn't annoying me, it made me question where we were going as a human race, emphasising the contrast between our natural environment and mankind's technological achievements, although in this case designed for killing people. Why do we suppose that "Peace" can only be attained by fighting for it? I found that the most powerful thing in life is love, it's amazing what lengths you'll go to when you love someone.

In the open fields there were few landmarks to mark our way but navigation was fairly easy making for a wonderful relaxing day. The only surprising map reference was Robin Hoods Grave so we stopped at a mound of earth where presumably some man, if not *the* man, who once acted nobly, was buried. I couldn't explain it, it just felt like a solemn place so, showing respect for the departed, decided this wasn't the place to break out the sandwiches and moved on.

Music: Chopin—Nocturne In E Flat Major, Op.9 No.2

Orton appeared in the distance and as we looked down on the small village I was thinking there was a danger we'd be there before the pub opens. A striking and unmistakable feature of Orton is the Church with its white tower, so with this landmark set in our sights we confidently headed towards it. Our entrance was not quite the one I expected, the footpath leading over a high wall dropping us right into the cemetery as if to say "welcome to Orton".

Whenever I find myself walking through such a place I have an irresistible urge to read the tombstones. Ages, names and family names soon form images, rightly or wrongly, of their lives centuries ago.

The door was open and we were drawn into the Church, a convenient bench near the entrance provided a place to leave outside that which was not appropriate inside, so we left all our dirty things, rucksacks, sticks, on the bench, and took our muddy boots off before going inside, I felt pretty dirty myself but thankfully people like me are welcome, we found ourselves all alone in All Saints Church. I found three 17th Century bells in a frame with informative notes about their history which somehow interested me. As we left I exchanged a donation for a post card to send to mum. We sat on the church bench looking at the views, we had nothing to do and all the time to do it, something precious and difficult to find in our busy working lives. I was so relaxed I became concerned that my metabolic rate would drop dangerously low and I might not recover so I felt the urge to get up again.

Venturing into the small village we found a Post Office. Excited, not having looked into a shop window for over a week, I struggled to decide what to look at. I normally go to a shop for a specific item, but here on display was everything one needed including pies and pipe tobacco. I looked at Deborah to try and get her attention then waved my post card indicating I would be going in to buy a stamp, but she hadn't noticed me, her eyes too were distracted. When she finally looked back I suggested we could buy some food here, a cooked chicken, cheese, bread, bottle of wine, make sandwiches for our dinner and if they have them some plasters. I was poised ready, "that's a good idea" she said, and at her nod I forcefully grabbed the door handle failing to come to an embarrassing halt with my face on the glass. Only then I noticed, an inch from my nose, the sign "closed for lunch", how quaint I thought, shops actually closing for a lunch break. Not to worry though, a 10 minute stroll around the village and it would be open again. Having passed 10 minutes strolling though the village observing the architecture of a bygone era we returned with hungry enthusiasm to purchase local produce for our dinner.

Arriving in the graveyard at Orton

Did you know rucksacks become part of your body after many hours perched on your back to the point that you can forget they are there? In a confined space, suddenly feeling the urge to turn around with delight to inform the wife of the abundant choice in local cheeses, this happened causing a carousel of birthday cards to come crashing to the ground. Realising that saying "hello" and smiling wouldn't exonerate me from the crime, I thought it was wise to make a discrete exit in reverse leaving the wife to safely do the shopping preferring to wait patiently outside.

To me this seemed a strange place for a Chocolate Factory but right in the centre of the village there it was, a true cottage industry, Kennedys Chocolate Factory. How could I leave my wife to wonder about all alone? No I must accompany her to see what this is all about and try to understand why anyone would pay so much for a single chocolate. Still wearing our boots which were now not so muddy, as most of it we'd left in the post office, we boldly marched in. To ensure customers stay a while to view the manufacture and contemplate purchasing an assortment beyond financial belief, they have a little café nestled, or should that be Nestléd, like a goldfish bowl in the centre of production. We sat down and secured our rucksacks out of harms way, a rest for me to tell the truth, whilst observing liquid chocolate being poured into all sorts of moulds.

Two home made soups consumed at pensioners pace were a fair price for our rest and, accompanied with a wonderful warm bread roll, made an adequate meal in itself with no need at all for a chocolate desert. I was surprise the wife was able to resist. Having discussed the events of our day and plans for the rest of it I felt our parking ticket had ran out, I confess I succumbed to having a dozen hand made little darlings wrapped and sent to my mum, hopefully to be shared out on our return.

Music:Enrique Granados, Op 37. No. 5, Danza Espanola

Staring at the George Hotel, our resting place for the night and the only pub in the village, there was no sign of life and no other option but to wait. Fortunately there was a bench to sit on so, rather then walking around aimlessly, we sat and stared. After a while a school bus arrived and four school children jumped off loudly, one of them accurately tossing an empty drinks bottle in the bin next to our bench. I had to hold my breath to avoid asphyxiation by the bus as it pulled off leaving a dense cloud of engine smoke behind then wait a further 5 minutes before the noise died down as the kids slowly dispersing into the village. Just as I thought peace had returned I was buzzed by an angry wasp followed by a swarm of the little devils that had been attracted by the discarded drinks bottle, in fear of being stung I suddenly jumped up and started doing a crazy little dance.

At last a van came down the lane and stopped outside the pub, I thought our bags had arrived and they had. We stayed put, allowing another 10 minutes to pass then, adopting a casual stroll as we approached, decided to go and book in. There wasn't much formality, we were clearly the first to arrive and we ended up with a large room, which looked back out at the seat we were sat on earlier. I decided to rate the room against my walkers B&B criteria, it had an en suite, albeit the size of a passage way, the loo paper was a bit thin but laundry facilities and the heated towel rail made the overall score a respectable one.

Having lots of time on our hands we made most of the facilities taking the opportunity to wash all our socks and underwear hanging it on the towel rail to dry. I suggested to the wife she showered first, to check that the shower was functioning as one might expect, however as soon as I stepped in the water temperature began to rise uncontrollably, in complete contrast to my Patterdale experience, until I could bear it no more. I'd been steam cleaned and felt absolutely jiggered so I went to lay on the bed.

I opened my eyes to notice it was fairly dark outside, the curtains were still drawn, and there was a muffled noise from the room below which suggested people were in the bar drinking and being very merry. The wife had already manufactured some sandwiches with our local post office provisions so we stayed in the room to enjoy them. Eventually the noise from below, coupled with a fear of missing out, became a compelling urge to find out what was going on so off to the bar we went.

It was no surprise to find many of the walkers we'd already met were there and the noise was primarily due to fifteen Australians who'd rearranged the furniture so they could all sit together in a long line. Chris and few other familiar faces were also there but rather than butt into their established conversation we decided to order a pint and sat quietly at a table on our own.

The George had a layout to accommodate all with a dining room at one end, bar with pool table and dart board in the middle area, complemented by a TV showing sports channels at the other. We sat in the bar and had a couple of relaxing drinks whilst discussing the changing landscape, our various walking companions, my blister of course which had given me little trouble today, and our destination tomorrow, Kirkby Stephen.

Chapter 7

Thirteen miles today, that sounds reasonable I thought flexing my toes as I lay in bed looking at the rose coloured curtains illuminated by the morning sunlight suggesting it was another fine day. Thin curtains do have the benefit of ensuring you are awake early, a warm contented feeling surrounded me. I recalled my first visit to Paris, I was fourteen, and stayed in bed waiting for it to come light. I hadn't realised they'd closed the shutters, everyone wondered where I was, when I finally got up it was afternoon.

The time had come to get up and get on, I looked at the shower and hesitated being satisfied with a quick wash in the sink, the laundry was perfectly dry and within minutes we were packed and heading downstairs for breakfast. Not surprisingly last nights bar had become the dining room and we took a seat with the other guests and waited. A young chap wearing a white coat and a chequered hat rushed in carrying two hot plates acknowledging our presence with a brief "morning" as he passed by. One the way back he took our order and was gone. I thought this is just like the bus conductor and bus driver when the two roles were merged into one role and the driver also collected the money to save resources to everyone's detriment. This chap was taking orders, cooking it, serving it, cleaning up and doing a fine job of it I have to add, certainly enough to warrant a verbal complement from me on his poached eggs on toast. Maybe he had a vested interest in the pub, anyway it looked like one mad panic for two hours and then his days work was done.

My hope today was that Kirkby Stephen would, among other things, have a shop that sold plasters, I'd finally eked out what I had until now and this was definitely the last day. All togged up off we set, the first few miles were along a country lane taking us back to the route. We set off at a leisurely pace taking time to look at the map for any interesting landmarks but none leapt out. Orton Scar, an interesting dark rock feature, was on our left and dark clouds were approaching from the south, we'd enjoyed good weather so far and after a philosophical argument decided to remain cheerful come what may. We weren't on our own for long and after a while there they were, the boisterous group of Australians, so decision time came; do we hold back to let them pass or march on?

Deciding to put our foot down to leave the noise behind we took a short cut heading directly for our first landmark a Stone circle. Rather like the time we set off from the Greyhound in Shap this path was also not frequently used and we drifted a little allowing the Australian group to gain on us so we upped a gear and marched on. Another mile further and it was clear our strategy was not working so, as they say, if you can't beat them join them so we engaged in conversation, their first comment being "it looks like you know where your going so we are following you! Well that was clearly their first mistake as a hundred yards later we came to a locked gate covered in barbed wire. Being unprepared to accept the error I decided to boldly negotiate the obstacle, high jump style, only to come to grief lacerating my hand and thigh on the barbed wire but making it over the gate and walking onwards as if nothing had happened. All the others, Deborah included, turned around and walked back to find path we'd missed.

The landscape had noticeably changed from hills to flats but I'd been walking on at an angle for many miles now and my right heel was beginning to complain. I used this as an excuse to have a water stop and remove a sock to reveal the damage. Two more blisters on my right heel, bugger. My boot must have been loose and the quick march had taken its toll. There was nothing for it but to tighten the boot and continue, at least the noisy crowd was ahead so we would see them stop for lunch, then we could too and keep our distance. The contented feelings I'd enjoyed that morning had turned into one of frustration and self annoyance as we plodded on mile after mile until a distraction came in the form of a remarkable dry stone wall which deserved some thought. This white limestone wall was well over six foot high and went on for miles and miles, clearly constructed by some wealthy landowner. We must have walked alongside it for another hour or more, seeing no one, pondering why it was built until hunger set in and we started to think about lunch.

Descending an embankment to join a disused railway we came to a derelict old station house which, having no other use these days, provided something to hide behind whilst we had a pee, as needs must. As I was watering some nettles I kept looking round expecting someone to appear out of the blue, or someone come cycling along the old railway track as they do, but to my surprise there was no one about and, even more strangely, no sound at all.

After walking for ten minutes, the Australian group became clearly visible, about half a mile ahead presumably having stopped for their lunch, gathered in an idyllic spot on a little old stone bridge across a beck. Our timing was impeccable and as we approached we greeted one another then they finished their lunch and set off allowing us the same idyllic vantage point. For an engineer, like myself, the view of Scardalegill viaduct made my day. What an amazing piece of engineering it was and, being so remote, few people will ever set eyes on. I confess I hadn't done my homework and it came as a surprise to see it, time to bring the camera out for a photo of it and look at the map to see where we were exactly.

As a slight distraction, if you know anything at all about the history of railways you'll have heard of the Settle to Carlisle line. Well this railway we were crossing was its competitor in the early days of steam, now disused. When we've walked a few more miles we'll cross the Settle to Carlisle line before Kirkby Stephen. There would have been thousands of workers here shovelling and blasting the rock during its construction for which many lost their lives. I could picture the activity of the bygone era, I heard a horse was reversing a cart load of rock into a shaft when the cart went too far and dragged the horse down the shaft. It was too difficult to get out so they left it there. A hundred and fifty years later, although the story was known, it had been forgotten exactly where the tragedy happened. Recent developments in radar technology have been used to find an image of the horse's skeleton inside the shaft.

Still in reminiscing mode I wondered, with admiration, how Peter and Brenda, who had walked from Shap to Kirkby Stephen, in one day, had faired. David and Caroline, who were a day behind, should also be arriving in Kirkby Stephen today.

We had our lunch and moved on, climbing a hill that was insignificant relative to those we'd climbed on the first days of our walk but it brought the thoughts of my feet and plasters back to the forefront of my mind. Afterwards a pleasing amble brought us to the Settle Carlisle railway line under which we passed to enter a farm yard ankle deep in muck. The muck was contrasted by an excellent flock of Wensleydale sheep which made me think of food as I'm quite partial to Wensleydale cheese.

A couple of miles further on and we arrived in the high street and sat on the first bench we saw, somewhat pooped, to take out all the maps and information in search of our B&B. Thankfully we were heading in the right direction. It was gone 5 o'clock so when we saw the "Walking and Hiking" shop my excitement was immediately quashed as I thought it will be shut, it took an age to cross the busy road but it was worth it, the shop was open.

This looked to me exactly like what a proper walking shop should look like, so I was in and sat down before saying hello explaining all my problems to a plump, but knowledgeable, shop keeper. Believing him to be a helpful man, on the basis he'd noticed I was wearing Bridgedale socks at a distance of 9 yards, I bought two new insoles and enough plasters to cover both feet. He said these plasters were the real McCoy, Compeed. I might have guessed they come in many different sizes so I had to fork out for several packs. Anyhow the process is apparently simple, just stick it on and leave it there until all is healed and it drops off. Leaving with renewed hope that I would be able to walk again we set off down the high street to locate our B&B, The Old Croft House. There it was, right in the centre of town and opposite was the Kings Arms, another great result!

Before making a bold entrance I hesitated for a moment outside the ornate wrought iron gate fronting the property, looking myself up and down to confirm that I was both muddy and rather smelly, a consequence of wading through the farmyard earlier. Recalling what Deborah had read about the B&B from the Guide Book earlier, we were about to step back in time to the 1900's and it seemed appropriate that I take some measures to please our host, I thought a good start would be to remove my boots. A jolly lady greeted us, telling me more than I knew about myself, and showed us our room insisting tea and scones would be sent up forthwith.

In terms of 1920's décor it didn't disappoint in the slightest, it was like stepping off the Orient Express into a Sherlock Homes period drama. The bathroom didn't disappoint either, there were all sorts of gadgets ladies would love, nail things, fancy hair dryer, foot spar, and enough smelly potions to mask out a zoo, and perhaps even me. Most importantly I noticed a piping hot radiator and thick loo paper too! Deborah was staring at the enormous cast iron bath when the scones arrived so she asked if was alright to run one, somewhat surprised, the lady thanked her for asking. I presume Deborah's thoughts were so immersed in the 1900's that hot water could not be taken for granted. I decided to pour the tea in a ritualistic manner which our surroundings demanded and enjoy the scones and cream, thankfully it wasn't pretend stuff squirted out of an aerosol can which would have certainly ruined the moment.

I also took the opportunity to soak in a real luxury bath tub then, with great excitement, opened the Compeed blister pack and, for once, decided to read the instructions to ensure I obtained the best result. I had now had a larger blister on the ball of my left foot and a row of small ones around the heel of my right foot. I was, I have to say, immediately impressed and relieved, which left me wondering do I have a lazy evening or do I put them to the test and go for a walk?

Our energy levels restored, thanks to the cream tea, we decided to stroll along the high street to find out what was going on and perhaps we might bump into someone we knew. We hadn't journeyed far; I was intently reviewing property details in an agent's window, when we heard a loud squawk causing us to look up. Behold there were three colourful birds flying over head. "Parrots" said Deborah, "Blue and Gold macaws" I said. I knew that because I once kept a parrot, it flew off one weekend when I left my dad to look after it and if you ever see one in the Bakewell area let me know. The Macaws were perched on a chimney pot, Deborah quickly rummaged for the only camera we had, her phone, and managed to captured the moment; colourful tropical birds on an old sooty chimney pot in a North Yorkshire town, that's one for the album.

It wasn't long before the old Kings Head beckoned us in for a pint, they know a thing or two about brewing beer in these parts, and sure enough there was a good choice of ales, a perfect place to spend the evening. Adjacent was a restaurant, we would have been happy with some bar food but the moment I asked it we could eat we were ushered in, still clinging onto my pint, and encouraged to take a seat. The restaurant was empty but I didn't mind so we took the opportunity to dine upmarket.

In true tradition we ordered the local Yorkshire cuisine and before it arrived the two elderly ladies Marg and Dot came in, greeted us with a subdued smile, and sat down. I checked to see if I was still covered in farmyard muck. Whether they'd seen us first or not I don't know but rather than sit close they chose a table some distance away, out of politeness I'd like to think. A conversation across the empty room developed, "how are you getting on", "did you see so and so" and "did you take a wrong turn at that sheep fold" . . . . within what seemed inane conversation an intimacy was developing as snippets of information begin to form a picture of each others lives rather like a jigsaw puzzle.

One thing left to clear up was the presence of the parrots, fortunately the waiter was able to enlighten us. Apparently there were 20 of the little darlings, who once belonged to some chap now deceased, essentially free to fly around and he'd left a fund for them to be cared for. They must know how good it feels to be free.

Replete we bid our farewells till the next day, happily paid the bill, and crossed the road to spend the night in the museum, rounding the evening off with an enjoyable night time chocolate as one would.

Farmyard Muck and Wensleydale Sheep

Chapter 8

The heavily lined curtains, from floor to ceiling, kept the room quiet and dark as morning broke allowing my body to gently ease into life at the start of another day. The shower temperature was controllable, which was another bonus, but I was in and out in a jiffy for fear of loosing a plaster. The laundry process was now seamless, just part of the morning ritual, helped of course by the excellent facilities, and there was time for once to take a good look at the map and see what was in store for us.

Today would be a mere thirteen mile hike over Nine Standards, which was a new one on me and warranted some research then, via four possible routes labelled different colours like red, blue, green on the map, a gentle decent to Keld. I immediately became inquisitive about the four route options, these depended on the time of year, or season, and then the penny dropped—we're talking peat bog, and our route today was right over the top.

Breakfast was plentiful and served without any hassle; I only ever saw the lady but presume someone else must be assisting in the kitchen. Two other couples joined us for breakfast, whom I judged to be none walkers, and finding nothing in common to share in conversation I returned to our room to pack.

A satisfied "goodbye" was exchanged on all sides and our exit was completed by the handing over of our packed lunch. In case we had to trudge through wet bog all day I wanted to wax my boots so sat on the door step outside and liberally sprayed away ensuring good coverage. It was soon apparent this was not a sensible place to do it. The wax I'd liberally applied was drying out turning the pathway to the B&B white and it looked horrible. Trying to scrub it in made matters worse so eventually I gave up "come on Deborah we're off" making a hasty and embarrassing departure.

After passing through a few narrow streets we left Kirkby Stephen behind and having crossed a bridge over the river took a moment to pause and reflect on our stay, wondering if I'd receive a bill for cleaning the path. Another mile or so gently passed then we started to climb. Within a short time Chris who must have been marching at twice our pace, caught us up. As we hadn't seen each other for a while there were things to discuss about the route, who we'd met and where we'd both stayed which developed into a detailed discussion about the day ahead, what the Nine Standards were, and how he agreed to meet "the others" there around 11.00 o'clock.

Conversation hadn't gone much further, we'd walked a couple of miles together, and it was clear to me that we were holding him back and he wanted to press on, so we said we'd see him later.

Stopping to take on water I suddenly exclaimed "I've left my walking stick behind!" I was amazed that I could allow myself to forget such a vital instrument, at which point Deborah also looked at her empty hands to say the same without actually voicing it. Yes we'd left our sticks behind. I suggested to Deborah to try her mobile phone, if there was a signal we could ask them to be sent on. Of all the days, this was going to be the one they would be most needed. As if by a miracle we received a signal, followed by a frantic search for the phone number, and a conversation to the lady who thankfully was there to answer the phone, explaining our memory loss. The van driver was just about to drive off with our bags and she managed to throw our sticks on the van. Phew, and not a mention of the white stuff all over her pathway which, thinking back, was the probably the reason why we'd left them. Off we set again, annoyed and surprised how we'd both come to forget our walking sticks, my body now feeling out of balance without it but, thankfully, still able to laugh.

The Nine Standards are, as you might expect, nine large stones which should be visible from miles away, I was expecting something a bit like Stone Henge. I kept a look out but the climb became rocky and we ascended into the cloud base, the temperature dropped, visibility was reduced to a few yards and the wind was blowing fine rain in all directions, even upwards. It all seemed to happen in a few minutes, no point in battling on without putting on our full wet weather gear for the first time in anger. There was nothing for it but to continue onwards and upwards, having never seen the Nine Standards before we might easily pass them by for all I knew, on a positive note I was certain we were on the right path.

At last we could see something that had to be the Nine Standards, what we could actually see were just two or three tall shadows in the fog, but yes we'd arrived at the Nine Standard and to greet us were everyone we'd ever met on our journey, all the Australians and more besides. Chris must have said we were on our way and thankfully they'd all waited for us. It was time to catch up with everyone, exchange experiences, and put some fuel in our bellies.

At the Nine Standards in Fog

After about 20 minutes an experienced sounding voice from the Australian camp suggested we set off. The route down looked as clear as mud, not surprising, in fact that was exactly what it was, we were in a serious wet peat bog. Someone had heard a lady had fell in and had to be pulled out by a tractor last week, seriously. The old wooden poles that had been used to mark the route must have been erected on a clear day and were too far apart for us to see the next one in the fog.

Which direction to take was, basically, a guess and our path randomly meandered through the foggy peat bog as we all tried to find firm ground. We were like frogs on a lilly pond all leaping from one island of heather to another surrounded by dark peat water. Now and then we struggled to find a way ahead, everyone becoming bunched up like sheep until someone was brave enough to take a run and jump onto something they hoped would hold their weight. If successful, first one, then another, would jump across until a landing party was assembled the other side, hands out stretched beckoning those behind to take a leap into the unknown.

Team work paid off, thanks to all, and a couple of hours later we were making our decent under blue skies and bright hot sunshine, no one would have believed the weather we'd had earlier had they not been there. We still had many hours of walking to do today, my feet were fine, it felt like we'd now done all the hard work and we could relax and enjoy the scenery. The wet bog had turned into a little stream, not "beck" we're in Yorkshire now, and I became fascinated to see the river Swale grow from a trickle to a stream as we started to follow it and would continue to do so for the next thirty miles.

The party was now beginning to thin out, perhaps because the danger was past and we no longer felt dependant on one another, I was chatting to David and Caroline who were sounding quite chipper when, suddenly, Caroline dropped like a stone as her foot got stuck in a small hole. I heard a "crack" as she fell and for a moment we all stopped as she rolled on her back grasping her leg in agony "it's broken, it's broken" she kept saying. David obviously tried to comfort her but her cries had attracted the attention of several nearby walkers who were now gathered in a circle around her, all looking at each other, thinking what would be the best practical thing to do.

After a couple of minutes she calmed down a bit and tried to put weight on her leg, which clearly said to me that it wasn't broken. One of the Australians, who sounded as though he'd been in this situation before, suggested she leave her boot on, rather than take it off, in case her foot were to swell up and it would never go back on. This led to a suggestion that she take some ibuprofen and paracetamol, at which point people started to look in their rucksacks, before long we had enough pills to open a pharmacy. A few minutes later she was helped to her feet but "hobbling" was the best way I could describe her progress. She was determined enough to carry on so several of us decided to accompany her at hobbling pace speaking words of encouragement. We walked together for about half an hour by which time she began to accept that she would not be able to complete the journey and at the next opportunity had resigned herself to accepting a lift to the hospital. David insisted we should carry on ahead and, with some hesitation but accepting there was nothing more that could be done, we did.

The next landmark was a Barn, in the absolute middle of nowhere, where they served tea and scones to passing walkers, such as ourselves. Still with thoughts of Caroline and David's disappointment in our minds we saw the Barn and followed the path to it coming upon a sign "free range children". The track to it became a ford across the Swale with a very old stone footbridge alongside. This was the eccentric English way of enjoying afternoon tea and scones, there were tables outside to sit at and not surprisingly the whole boggy team who crossed the Nine Standards earlier were already seated. A little dog came out barking as customers approached, not to ward them off, to alert the young mother who was serving tea to put the kettle on.

The young mother was indeed quite a character, so much so, it turned out her little business had been featured on TV. We sat with Chris, Marg, Dot and another couple we'd only just met looking out for David and Caroline. After an age, and two rounds of tea and scones, they appeared. Chris, being the gentleman, set off to greet them and returned carrying her rucksack.

Having explained the problem, the young mother dropped what she was doing, as if this was a frequent occurrence, put Caroline in the 4x4, and drove off to the Hospital saying she was a bit busy at the moment help yourself to tea and scones, leave the money in the box by the kettle.

For us there was still some walking to be done so we gracefully departed and continued to follow the Swale down stream stopping several times to take photos of deep red peat coloured waterfalls from old stone bridges on what, weather wise, turned out to be a glorious afternoon. An hour later the 4x4 came past driven by the young mother who give us a loud wave indicating Caroline had been safely delivered to Hospital. The last few miles were a peaceful stroll as the afternoon went cool coinciding with our timely arrival in Keld.

Keld is, well, not easy to describe. I took the map out to locate our lodgings for the night, we walked along the road coming to a sign Keld indicating we'd arrived then half a mile later Keld indicating we'd left. I only saw half a dozen buildings, nothing newer than 400 years old and there was no sign of any inhabitants whatsoever.

This was the half way mark, I was expecting a line across the road and flags waving but no, this was the most understated event you could imagine. The sign for our B&B was not conspicuous and we walked passed it twice having done two circuits round the tiny hamlet, the centre of which was an old red phone box, before deciding this must be the place and knocked on the door. There was a friendly greeting as we entered a booking in area, come boot room, where all the muddy wet gear was left together with the bags which were all plied up. Looking at the amount of mud, clearly we were not the first to arrive.

The next question was "could we eat here tonight" to which the answer was, thankfully, a simple yes. The lady didn't seem to want to volunteer what was on the menu and being prepared to eat almost anything I didn't ask. We negotiated our way along the narrow farmhouse corridors to a small room but very walker friendly, complete with heated towel rail and fantastic uninterrupted view across the Yorkshire dales, I opened the window, checking for sheep, so we could enjoy the fresh Yorkshire air.

As the hour approached seven o'clock we descended to find the lounge, we passed the kitchen to find Mr of the house busy cooking and, whatever it was, it smelt good. The lounge had a TV and newspapers on a centre coffee table surrounded by enough comfy sofas to seat ten or more. It was the first time I'd seen a television for over a week so I sat and looked at the news for a while until the lady came in and asked us if we wanted a drink. It turned out they have my favourite bitter on draught so I had to order a pint which arrived very promptly. I sat quite content, browsing thought the papers, during which time one or two other walkers of a similar disposition joined us. It turns out there are only two B&Bs, actually farmhouses, in Keld. Both are owned by the same family and the only people who ever stay are walkers. We were in Butt house, the Australian group was too big to fit in so, by process of elimination, they must be in Keld House.

Dinner was finally announced, there was a table set for six and one for four, the lady pointed at the one set for four and we sat down. The six arrived a couple of minutes later clearly a family group, as they all knew one another. They were doing the walk but we'd never seen them before. Then a young couple, also on the walk, joined our table. We didn't have long to wait and, after a quick introduction to Paul and Carla, the food started to arrive, and what cracking grub this was. I beginning to become accustomed to this informal way of living when, to top it all, a chap on the other table got up, directed his voice into the kitchen saying "alright if I help myself" and started pouring a pint, I thought, Simon old son, you've finally arrived I can cope with this.

Deborah so liked the pudding she asked for the recipe but the lady refused to give away her secrets. I have to say it was the best food I'd had for ages, we were all well fed, watered and satisfied. There was time to discuss the days that lay ahead with Paul and Carla, a knowledgeable Yorkshire couple, over a final pint, or two, before staggering upstairs falling into bed, watching the night stars appear before sleep stole the day.

Chapter 9

The thing about good beer is the lack of a hangover so my day started with the conclusion that what I drank last night must have been good. Having come to that astounding decision I leapt up out of bed, the wife gave me that look of surprise and disbelief at my bright cheery mood, and danced into the bathroom and on into the shower for some invigorating cleansing, having almost forgotten about all the plasters stuck to my feet. Deborah greeted me with a cup of tea as I came out of the shower but she still hadn't spoken, I said "if last nights food was anything to judge by then breakfast was not to be missed, bring it on" she remained silent which I took to be an indication that she was not well pleased with my behaviour last night.

On leaving, to finalise our bill, the lady simply asked how many pints I'd had. I warmed to this trusting approach with an inner smile, it could have great merit provided one remains sober enough to actually remember, fortunately on this occasion I had my wife to remind me. Our stay at Butt House was over, and I regret not having asked the meaning of its name, but our stay was a very enjoyable one. "Let us not forget the sticks" I said to Deborah, trying to muster up the courage to venture outside into the heavy drizzle that greeted us that morning, knowing there was no going back.

A final farewell and off we set, zipping up all plastic waterproofs which occupied me for the first 300 yards, trying to achieve the best comfort in a claustrophobic cocoon and not caring a bit what anyone thought of my appearance. It was the first time we'd set off in the full wet gear. It was getting a good test and I was thankful it was working as advertised, but it required effort and hindered my natural movement which was distracting.

If I wanted to hear what was said I had to let the hood down, if I tried to look behind me the persistent rain required that the hood remained up so rather than get wet I chose not to converse.

A simple 11 mile walk to Reeth lay before us this day and a choice of routes. The Swale flows to Reeth and following it would take us past a few villages on route with the potential to refuel at a tearoom or two. The other option was the high road north to old Lead Mine workings with place names such as Hard Level Gill, Gunnerside Beck (oops I was wrong earlier they do say Beck here, it must be Force and Spout that's changed) and Old Gang Lead Smelting Mill.

The low cloud indicated visibility would not be good so we decided on the low route. I kept looking for evidence of human habitation or something that could justify a purpose for the beautiful hamlet of Keld but, after a few minutes walking, we'd left Keld behind still mystified why it had some into existence in the first place.

The rain continued as we began following a tree lined beck, a northern rain forest good for the parrots perhaps, trying to keep an energetic pace and our spirits up, conscious that today could end up a dismal trudge. The woodland scenery now became the main focus of our attention, actually it was providing the only diversion, the industry of long ago had been completely softened by nature so I started to conjure up a picture of what the area might have looked like at the peak of our busy industrial revolution.

The weather sometimes looked like it was going to change but it didn't and our route, as pretty and scenic as it was, continued to follow the damp tree lined river being extremely muddy and sometimes completely waterlogged. For the first time we encountered people, a father and son, who had decided to tackle the Coast to Coast the other way. We were staring at each other across a waterlogged stretch of the path working out how to cross it and the situation instigated conversation. I felt a bit like Robin Hood meeting Little John. I could sense they were on a mission, and I was right for once, the father and son team were also doing the same route as ourselves but were tackling it in the opposite direction. I'd like to think it was a very welcome encounter for all, helped by their joyful expression and desire for enthusiastic discussion, which helped lift my spirits and raised a completely different subject to discuss as we walked on. I asked Deborah how would we get on if we were walking to the North Pole and never met anyone to cheer us up? Perhaps that could be our next walk?

The hours squidged by and without the need to look at my watch I heard my stomach indicating it was time for lunch. We were near "Low Row" which had a blue beer glass icon on the map indicating the presence of an Inn. I stared at the map through water was dripping off my hood and thought, if we stopped, we'd never get going again so kept quiet suggesting we briskly move on.

At that point on the route we came to a road, wide enough for two cars to pass but there was hardly any traffic, so decided to walk along it as a welcome change to the, now tiresome, boggy option. A tree up the roadside bank looked like it would provide some shelter so we headed for it. There were some temporary traffic lights indicating some repairs must be taking place but there were no workmen about so I figured they must have been on their lunch break too. We sat under the tree.

It was a contemplative day; I certainly hadn't expected to find myself here sat under a tree in the rain eating my sandwiches. I didn't feel there was a rush to get anywhere, there was no one about, we hadn't even met anyone we knew and my mind went blank not caring where we were going or why we'd even started our journey.

After about ten minutes silence I verbally concluded "they must have all taken the bus or the other route". Our cold bottoms were a good reason to rise to our feet and our limbs soon loosened and warmed up after the quick decent down the bank. Returning to the suggested route in our guide book we crossed the river Swale by an old stone bridge to the south bank. The river was now a significant force, we'd seen its birth from the top of boggy Nine Standards from a trickle, then a beck, and now here it was carving its way through rock. An unusual feature suddenly presented itself by way of a high wall between the river and a large open field, clearly built to prevent flooding, just the width of one paving stone it had become the path itself. I have to say negotiation was a bit unnerving made worse by the very wet slippery conditions.

Wondering if we'd ever get there today I started to look out for landmarks to determine our exact whereabouts and calculate the time remaining, another indication of how interesting the wet day had been. I identified a farm and, using our average speed so far, calculated we should arrive around 3 o'clock that afternoon. That should give us plenty of time to book into the B&B and dry out before the evening.

Music: Gymnopedie no3 by Erik Satie

Waterfall near Keld

Finally we came to signs of habitation, a dirt track which turned into a street, some old houses and at last, just as the weather started to break, we arrived in Reeth, boasting two pubs a few shops, café and several B&B's, what more could we want? The shops thrived on busloads of folk who come here because "All Creatures Great and Small" was filmed here.

That day our arrival coincided with the end of the village market, at least that's what I concluded as I saw a butcher looking chap loading legs of beef onto a van parked on the village green. The café looked like it was still open and had two seats outside so we took off our soggy rucksacks and parked our bottoms. I watched the butcher man drive off then started searching for our cash. After much searching I entered the café brandishing a dry ten pound note. Trying not to drip mud everywhere I walked on tiptoe the full length of the shop to be greeted by some mouth watering cakes and a shop assistant with a bemused expression stood behind the counter. There seemed little point attempting to exchange pleasantries "two teas and two large slices of that ginger cake" I said. "I'll bring them out to you" was the reply, and with that I tiptoed back outside.

There we sat in the drizzle with a cup of tea and a very tasty ginger cake having one of those people watching moments, but without many people. A young couple with a pram circled round a few times, I couldn't decided if they were just window shopping or were wondering where the market was then they came over towards us. I was about to say "I think the market has packed up and gone" when the young lass asked if we knew anyone called Robin and Tricia? Blimey, turned out it was their daughter, with grandchild in the pram, having come to greet them at Reeth. I admit to being somewhat surprised and reassured them that if they are not already here they won't be far behind us. She left looking happier and a few minutes later the united family returned to say hello and share their delight as it was the first time Robin and Tricia had seen their granddaughter. On that happy note we agreed to meet in the pub for dinner that evening, but which one? Reeth has two pubs; the Black Bull and the Kings Arms Hotel, the Black Bull with ale from Masham was the choice for me.

Feeling too cool for comfort we decided it was time to walk again and find our B&B for the night which had the grand name of Arkelside Country

Guest House and, according to the guide book, boasted stunning views across Arkle beck. Due to the very low cloud all that was irrelevant, all I actually needed was a hot shower and bed for the night, a heated towel rail would be a bonus of course. This time our B&B was tucked away down a little cul-de-sac and took some finding, being weary didn't help. A friendly greeting awaited us, although our room looked a little poky it didn't disappoint with regard to the facilities, and within the hour there I was looking at the view of clouds from our window, warm and dry, towel rail duly employed for our daily laundry. All was well apart from Deborah's knee, which had decided to give her some trouble at the end of this our ninth day.

Although Reeth is a relatively small town I recalled seeing a sign for a new outdoor walkers shop, it wasn't quite yet closing time and so, with little else to do, we set off in the vain hope of finding a knee support bandage device. The shop was indeed new and to my surprise open, it looked like we were inside a converted barn with all its glorious high wooden beams and prices to match. After browsing for five minutes Deborah suddenly produced the perfect item to support her knee, to my utter amazement. I was so pleased for her, I experienced similar delight when discovering "Compeed" the consequence of which had made my walking so much more enjoyable. Beaming with delight, if a little lighter in pocket, we left the outdoor walkers shop with the knee support employed and functioning satisfactorily.

Alright, I admit it was a bit early, but we were actually passing the pub door so I thought we should pop in for a pint whilst waiting for the others. This looked like a great old pub, a good feeling with a fireplace large enough to roast an ox. Why was I surprised to find we shared a mindset with folk we'd walked many a mile with? I'd been beaten to it. At the bar was a couple who were at Buck House in Keld, a couple of Australians, Robin and Tricia, David and Caroline, and Chris. This was clearly the right place for a walkers rendezvous. The couple at the bar clocked us and he, another Chris, asked what we were drinking. Before the second pint arrived everyone was outpouring their stories starting with Caroline who was by now displaying her very colourful but badly bruised ankle on the table, around which we had all congregated, justifiably seeking sympathy because her journey had ended prematurely.

After much discussion over another pint Fish and Chips were ordered and over the next pint Chris told his story: His accommodation was the pub next door which had a bathroom down the corridor. He'd had a few drinks by now so admitted to everyone his earlier mistake of taking a shower having forgotten to take his room key. The bathroom door closed behind him and he found himself stuck in the corridor wearing only his pants. The solution to his predicament was to go into the crowded pub, wearing just his underpants, and ask for another room key which, for some reason no one could explain, took a very long time to come.

The Fish and Chips were well above par, mushy peas included, and simply had to be washed down with more beer but afterwards, in a more serious mood, thoughts turned to tomorrow and the 11 mile walk to Richmond. Concluding that we would all benefit from a good nights sleep, immediately Deborah stood up and so we left limping back to our B&B, realising the beer although a good aesthetic, had not actually cured our injuries. After a rainy day it was good to let our hair down.

Chapter 10

I 'm sure I heard the rain dripping off the gutter during the night. You know the sensation when you're neither awake nor asleep but aware of what's going on although unwilling, or unable, to doing anything about it. None the less, most of the time between going to bed and waking up had to be attributed to sleep and I was blessed with a shower that was neither too hot nor too cold just right in fact.

The breakfast room had an exposed stone wall along one end and massive windows with views across to Arkle Beck. There was one other resident at breakfast, turns out she'd come for a wet weekend break and hadn't seen Arkle Beck either. The Fish and Chips had been well digested by now and I was ready for my poached egg on toast but disappointed to find it was tainted with vinegar. I'd seen the same cookery program on TV on how to poach an egg: A pan of water is brought nearly to the boil, a pinch of salt and a splash of vinegar is added, it's stirred to form a whirlpool then the egg is dropped in. Well on this occasion the amount of vinegar was too much for me and I couldn't eat it. Never mind, I thought there's no point in wasting time moaning about it, we have some walking to do so lets grab our packed lunch and get on with it!

Feeling fully prepared for the day ahead, me with two layers of socks and Deborah with her new knee support, we boldly set off. At least it wasn't raining at the moment but there were some ugly looking clouds drifting over us threatening a shower. They served as a constant reminder to keep an eye on the weather in case the need arose to quickly don the plastic waterproofs. After walking a mile down a hill, leaving the little town of Reeth behind, we came alongside our old friend the river Swale. The landscape was pretty, but much different to the hilly days at the start of our journey, don't get the impression that the days ahead were less demanding, perhaps the sense of achievement wasn't quite the same. Although certainly not boring, was this daily repetition sapping my enthusiasm I wondered? Did I need rejuvenating?

Music: Gabriel Faure's Pavane, Op. 50

Ahead I could hear Australian banter and turning round Chris could be seen approaching at full speed. I didn't feel we needed the same team work as the Nine Standards demanded, I was after just a gentle stroll today with my wife, but once again it wasn't to be. A description in the Guide Book had puzzled me that morning and we'd just reached the point on route where, according to the guide book, we are suppose to turn up hill like a "Startled Badger". I was struggling to imagine what was meant by that expression, most badgers I've seen are flat in the road, although we did see a mother and her cubs playing in our garden once, that was a delight.

We were all stood there wondering which way to turn but could see no obvious route. The Australians had already fanned out in search of the route ahead and one of them suddenly announced he found it. I was so thankful again for the time and effort this saved us, I didn't want another detour adding potentially adding miles to my day. The route became somewhat non descript and I found myself drifting across open fields with an old stone barn in each one. Conversation also dried up and reasons why I was there started to surface, but not because of any pain from the blisters or fatigue today. I think I'd reached the stage where the normal routine of life, the day to day going to work and all that, could be completely forgotten and put aside allowing more important issues in life to be given serious consideration, starting with thoughts like we should be human beings rather than the humans doing.

Approaching an old barn I stopped to stare at the dark rain cloud which was now heading our way. Deborah reached for her water proofs and I took the opportunity to remove the water flask from my rucksack for a drink and stood watching the cloud for several minutes while some straggling Australians passed by. I felt the necessity to speak and explain why I'd stopped so I casually said to the last passer by "I'm just watching that rain cloud to see if it's coming our way". "You stay there and keep an eye on it and I'll carry on . . . ." he said in an Australian accent his words dying out as he continued to pass by eventually becoming inaudible.

It was just what I needed to spur me on, some people are spectators and some are participators and I wasn't here to be one of life's spectators. I said nothing to Deborah but as soon as the Australians were gone we set off eagerly finding ourselves ten minutes later running to a lonesome beech tree for cover, laughing out loud uncontrollably, as the heavens opened and it started to poor down.

There was the confirmation; life isn't interesting just watching what's going on, you need to get involved. It was as good a time as any to eat our sandwiches and wait for the sunshine to return, which it did. The rolling countryside may not seem interesting but there is always evidence of habitation and a mystery to be unravelled of why and how people live their lives if you look for it.

Early afternoon brought a pleasant surprise in the form of Chris who was walking back towards us. He explained he'd gone wrong and must have missed a turning, so he was retracing his steps. Back on track we all set off together arriving at a small village bold enough to have a sign "Tea Room" which we decided to follow. It led us to a lovely garden with a conservatory large enough for about a dozen covers and a log burner to welcome customers on a cold day.

Relieved to see that it was open, evident by the fact that there appeared to be two customers already seated, spirits rose at the thought we'd soon be able to enjoy a cup of hot tea, and hopefully a piece of cake, so we removed boots, ventured in and sat down. After some time a lady, speaking in a tone like a church wardens wife, came to take our order. After a painfully long time the lady returned with a pot of tea then immediately disappeared again. Some time later the milk arrived and we all looked at one another without verbally surmising what the problem might be. Two more customers arrived and sat down, she returned, took their order and went again but we still hadn't got our piece of cake.

Clearly she was on her own but only capable of processing one order at a time, as we weren't in a hurry it wasn't a problem, I was just becoming inquisitive. The next time she returned there was a party of four more customers standing waiting, but there was no table available that could seat that many. The lady was flummoxed and began to panic. Chris was sat at the end of our table, which meant there were three of us at a table that could seat four, and the last two customers were also sat at a table for four. There were two tables that could seat two which were empty. She came to a solution and pointed at Chris, announcing "could you sit over there, indicating he should sit on his own at a table for two, then two of these people could sit here and two could sit there". Completely bemused by her logic Chris decided to oblige in order to make her life easy. She took another order from those that had just been seated and left again. The situation was becoming amusing for those who'd been there for more than 10 minutes and had seen what was happening. Then the party of Australians arrived. How we'd passed them I don't know, I presume they'd taken shelter in a Barn during the rain. By the time the lady returned the group of Australians had finished taking off all their muddy boots and hanging their waterproofs on the garden furniture and were entering the conservatory looking for somewhere to sit.

At this point she flipped shouting out it wasn't possible for her to serve so many people, normally there are only one or two people who come in for a cup of tea. In a very polite way she told all her customers to emphatically go away . . . . I'd never seen anything like it, I also felt a little sorry the Australians who wanted to enjoy an English afternoon tea. Chris smiled from where he was sat announcing he was in the naughty boys chair and hadn't got his cake yet, we left the money for what we'd had on the table and departed.

We walked with Chris again, discussing the amusing Tea Room event, sharing our life stories over several miles. He was a retired plumber from Eastbourne, he was walking on his own and his wife would be waiting to greet him at the end of the walk. We passed the party of Australians who had rested to refuel so we exchanged greetings, I just stopped short of apologising for what happened in the tea room. Chris decided he would stop for a bite to eat and we took this to mean he wanted a rest from our natter.

The weather had turned in our favour; it had stopped raining and was beginning to brighten up, we should have a good afternoon. Richmond came into view as it should and we started our long decent to greet it, the Castle clearly visible for miles. I'd never been there before but it had a welcome feeling about it. It was the main town on route so we expected shops and restaurants although we were not in desperate need of anything. We navigated into the town centre to find the two Australian ladies Liz and Helen, whom we'd met on day two, window shopping. Dressed in all their brightly coloured walking kit they stood out from the crowd like Chapel hat pegs, "tourists!" I said, intended as a friendly greeting.

Deborah and I did a couple of circuits of the town square looking at the market stalls and the arrival of a Bride and Groom outside the main hotel. "It must be Saturday" I said, this must also be one of the first times we'd been twice round a town and not bought anything. Saturday or not we decided to eat out that night but first we needed to find the Old Brewery B&B which meant descending a narrow cobbled street down a rock face.

Naturally, finding the Old Brewery didn't present a problem for me. It seemed an efficiently run place, our bags were waiting and the room was one of the best we'd had in all respects, the window opening onto a little courtyard where the late afternoon sun invited guests to sit outside and take tea.

I'd noted several watering holes as we passed through town earlier, some worthy of closer inspection later for dinner and a pint. Having plenty of time it seemed like a good idea to explore Richmond a little and walk around the Castle wall which rose up steeply from the banks of the Swale, so we spent some time exploring the old town.

The first pub we went in looked inviting from the outside but after ordering a pint I began to regret going in, the smell of old beer and cooking was embedded in the fabric, this wasn't the place I wanted to take my wife so we moved swiftly on. The main hotel in the market place, where we saw the Bride and Groom arrive earlier, was now deserted. There was no one at the bar or in the restaurant so that didn't look very inviting either.

I felt sure we should see the others somewhere about, if anything the Australians should be audible. We looked in two or three restaurants but saw no one we knew and became very indecisive about where, or what, to eat. There was a small supermarket still open so we decided to buy some provisions for the next day and a bag of crisps and chocolates to enjoy that night.

We could see one place that was doing good trade, and many cars were pulling up outside, a Pizza Kebab take away. As we walked past the smell caused us to pause, we looked at one another thinking "why not?" Deborah said it was the best Pizza she'd had as we sat on a closed shop doorway tucking into our takeaway, observing the youngsters driving their cars with loud exhausts. Full of enjoyable grease and dough we had one more look in a pub, hoping to see someone we knew, to no avail. Quizzical and slightly disappointed we decided to give up and returned to the Old Brewery for an early night.

Today required patience and perseverance, two qualities I struggle with, expecting a result when I want one,

Chapter 11

I'd slept like a log. A glimpse out of the window suggested we were in for a fine day so I was eager for an early start and a good breakfast. Danby Whiske was our next destination, a 14 mile walk ahead of us, I recall Chris saying there's a fair stretch along the road so he was going to wear his trainers. No I thought I'll stick with what I know, my boots and two layers of socks. It's taken a lot of trial and error over many miles to get this comfortable. I took a leisurely hot shower and renewed all my plasters for good measure.

Down we went for breakfast and took a seat. Looking around there were two other couples, I'd never seen before, they all seemed to be waiting for food to arrive. We weren't in much of a rush so I studied the menu debating with myself what to have, eventually the full English was too tempting to resist so I mentally rehearsed what I wanted, just to ensure I'd remember to add Black Pudding and fried mushrooms. Perhaps, if I'd not been given much time to think about it I would have ordered my usual, healthier, eggs on toast but I hate being predictable.

A very polite and shy young lady came out with a plate of full English and placed it in front of a man sat on the next table, one glance and that confirmed what I wanted. She came to take our order and returned to the kitchen. After some time the manager stormed through the dining area straight into the kitchen and closed the door behind him, thinking we wouldn't hear what was said. It sounded like the cook still hadn't turned up for work so he was forcefully asking the young lady, who was actually the cleaner and had already done her job, to carry on and do breakfast.

In a bizarre way this was reminiscent of the tea room experience we had yesterday. She took just one order then went back into the kitchen to cook it, when it was cooked she brought it out, took another order and went back into the kitchen again. This was the longest breakfast we'd waited for, at one point a chap came in and asked if his packed lunch was ready yet, she apologised saying she hadn't got round to it yet, he responded I can't wait any longer I've got 20 plus miles to walk today, I'm off. I was thankful we'd bought our provisions at the Coop yesterday so we didn't have to wait for our packed lunch.

When breakfast did arrive it was very good, she'd done her very best under the circumstances and deserved some credit. As we checked out the manager was very apologetic, to add to his troubles the Sherpa van had also broken down that morning so he was wondering how to transport the bags. It wasn't the end of the world but he was so wound up I felt he needed a little prayer to bring peace and joy into his life that day. I also mentioned how good breakfast was.

A look at the map indicated another milestone today, we would be crossing the A1 near Catterick Racecourse. The first part of the route took us via the back of some houses and allotments at the south end of Richmond and required constant referral to the guide book to ensure each gate and left and right turn was accurately followed for fear of ending up in someone's back yard, or worse not ending up on the right road out of town. The best way to leave Richmond behind was indeed by road for the first couple of miles until we passed the sewage works then we took a lane on the left to follow the Swale again, which no longer had the same appeal. By now I wanted to stop for a pee but we were constantly plagued with joggers, for some reason the path along the Swale was a popular route and it was a good while before we were certain we were alone again. Two thoughts came to mind at this time; there a long way to go and the full English breakfast was not the best option to start the day.

All the guide books tell you about it, well all those I'd read before starting this walk, and now I know why. Carbohydrates are best for a walker's breakfast, not a full fry up, but I'd succumbed to the irresistible smell of fried bacon which I now realise was a big mistake. I should have stuck to the eggs on toast.

Confusion arose at a crossroads, actually an intersection of five footpaths, which was not at all clear on the map. We took our best guess and fortunately I'd only gone a few 100 yards before I realised we taken the wrong one, deciding it would be best to retrace our steps so we did, there were no Australians or team work this time, we were on our own. I'd heard the Australians were staying in Richmond for an extra days rest, or drinking, which was why I expected to find them celebrating in town last night and easy to find.

Brompton-on-Swale was in view on the other side of the river and as we approached it we met Robin and Tricia sat on a log in the corner of a field, Tricia with her phone pressed firmly to her head thinking out loud. We could see she was deeply engrossed so we decided not to stop and made do with waving friendly gestures at Robin who replied. Another couple of miles and we were clambering down a muddy embankment to walk under the A1 road bridge, I paused to look at the concrete structure with thoughts similar to those I had when crossing the M6, plus all the other events on route we'd endured to get here. Crossing the A1 was another major milestone for me.

We emerged the other side of the A1 to find ourselves at a busy event at Catterick race course. Not wishing to stop we moved quickly on crossing a busy road and a bridge over the Swale to follow it on the other bank. The route was becoming disjointed, a dog leg here then a dog leg there, a bit of road then a field, another bit of road and then another field, until we found ourselves on a road with several miles hiking to do. It was a B road and we didn't see a car for hours but walking on tarmac became less and less enjoyable as the miles went on and on.

It's a Crossroads alright but is it clear where your heading?

There was only one interesting moment so I stopped to take the camera out and photograph an old signpost, which certainly hadn't seen a lick of paint since the war, at a cross roads on our way to Danby Whiske. We were walking in open countryside with a big sky on a fine day but being on the tarmac my knee joints were starting to suffer from the constant jolt on the hard surface. Relief finally came when I saw Chris sat outside the pub at Danby Whiske, a most welcome sight indeed.

I headed straight into the bar, bought the wife and I a drink of course, and came out to join him. The comforting thing was that Chris admitted he'd also gone wrong at the 5 way crossroads but had carried on to the next village before he was able to get back on track, clearly he'd done several extra miles, mind you he set off before us, not having to wait so long for his breakfast helped. He was now waiting for a lift to his B&B, it wasn't really cheating, that's reasonable if you can't get accommodation right on the actual route. They'll often collect you and return you to the same point the next day at no extra cost to get the business. Our accommodation was on route but looking at the map told me we still had several miles to walk. It was a Farmhouse and miles from civilisation so we would be relying on them to provide our evening meal which they advertised.

Just the one pint and then onwards we must go. I noticed a footpath taking us exactly where we wanted to be so rather than keep walking on the road I suggested we take it. As soon as we'd crossed the mainline London to Edinburgh railway, we turned off to find this was another one of those footpaths rarely used, necessitating some wading through brambles. As we passed near a farm, not the one we were looking for, we heard a dog barking and immediately thought we were the cause, not at all an unusual event but the dog kept on barking then this sheepdog began running towards us. Fortunately it turned out not to be vicious so we figured it was just bored, as not many people walk this way, and wanted to play. A mile later it was still following us as we reached another farm, all our attempts to send it back home had been to no avail. I was under the impression that Sheep dogs knew all about working with Sheep so, as we entered a field full of sheep, I thought the dog would be familiar with its surroundings and act sensibly but this turned out not to be the case. The dogs eyes opened wide, the sheep started to run, and in seconds it was like being in the middle of a merry-go-round at the fair, clearly the dog thought this is great fun whereas I could see who would be shouldering the blame. The game continued, the sheep leaping over fences and hedges in all directions, if ever there was just cause for shooting a dog this was it.

Feeling completely helpless we carried on walking, hoping the dog might follow us, after five minutes I looked back and could still see the chaos in the distance. A 4x4 car then came down a farm track towards us and stopped. I thought this is it, a young lad jumped out of the car and ran towards me but carried straight on past me shouting "Basil!" His mother stayed by the car looking concerned and as we approached she explained that he likes to follow walkers and ends up miles from home. I was left thinking this sheep dog might not like home or would benefit from a bit of training.

Another ½ mile to go, all up hill, and we would be there. It had been a 14 mile slog to Danby Whiske, plus a few extra miles to our Farmhouse B&B, which turned out to be miles from anywhere. It was a long ½ mile but finally we arrived, tired and weary, at our B&B. It was a working Farm, evident by the cattle we had to force our way past to get to the front door, and my first thought was, would I be kept awake all night by the animal noises?

The farmers' wife greeted us and, having taken one look at us, immediately directed us to the boot room. Obviously they had walkers in mind when deciding to diversify and do a B&B converting the old stable blocks into bedrooms. It looked quite modern inside suggesting the B&B business was a recent decision. The room was fine and lent itself to a much needed rest after, what in my book was, an arduous day on foot. Once our energy levels were sufficiently restored I thought we'd better ask about having dinner that evening, so we went in search of the farmer's wife.

The place had all the attributes and accoutrements one would expect in an old farm house and, where else would you expect to find a farmers wife, there she was stood cooking at the AGA. I thought she looked a bit surprised when we asked if we could have dinner there that night. They'd made specific reference to dinner being available in the brochure, or rather the folded up piece of paper that was in my pocket. She said most boarders take the bus into the next town but she could sort something out. There wasn't a choice on offer, it probably never crossed her mind to ask if we were vegetarians, and what would one expect on a working farm? Beef I suppose. It sounded like she was being put out, but we hadn't factored in any bus rides as part of our journey, she then directed us to the lounge where the two of us could sit and wait.

It was very peaceful so we sat there, just the two of us wondering where everyone else was staying. The best part of an hour past by then the Farmer himself came in, said a polite hello and indicated dinner would be ready soon so we could go though to the dining room. As we went in we were pleasantly surprised to find we were not alone, a sentiment shared by the two other ladies who were dining with us. Although we hadn't met before it was obvious we were all on the same journey so we struck up conversation without difficulty, being able to share similar thoughts about, well, dinner and walking.

I figured the Farmer had already eaten his dinner before beginning his duties as waiter. He brought in our dinner with a smile, we all looked at it and then at one another, all quietly thinking there's not very much of it. Beef it was and I could have eaten it again, thankfully, there was pudding to come. After making short work of the pudding, rather than dry up, conversation went a little deeper. One lady, Karen, revealing she was a police woman, now divorced. The other lady, her sister, revealed she worked in the health service but resisted going into more detail, perhaps she thought it might put me off my dinner. For a change there was no beer, no wine, no liquor coffee, just conversation a cup of tea then a welcome bed. I'm pleased Basil enjoyed his day.

Chapter 12

I was woken by early morning farmyard noises, a new experience but not too surprising given our location. It sounded like the farm animals were just outside our bedroom window. I told the wife I'd had a good night's kip and, despite the usual aches and pains, I was ready for the day ahead. Due to the extra few miles we did yesterday today was a short stroll to Ingleby Cross, a mere nine miles. "This should be the easiest day of them all" I exclaimed to Deborah, stopping abruptly as I drew back the curtains to see a large Frisian staring at me. "It's raining again" I said.

After much deliberation over the breakfast menu, and careful consideration of the consequences, I decided that will power would prevail and chose lots of carbohydrates with eggs on. "This will be a good day to test out our waterproofs", I kept telling Deborah enthusiastically, "haven't we been blessed so far with good weather . . . ." I contemplated asking for a packed lunch, trusting the farmer's wife would supply a wholesome farm food delight, but Deborah pointed out there was a village pub only 9 miles away so we resisted.

The two ladies we shared dinner with last night arrived for their breakfast just as we'd finished. The weather was the only subject of conversation which delayed us for just five minutes and then we left assuming our paths would cross later that day as we were all destined for Ingleby Cross.

Adorned in our full waterproof gear again, eager to leave the farmyard groaning noises and smell behind, we set off mindful that there were two plus points, namely the terrain was quite flat and it was not too windy, which made walking in the rain manageable, if not even pleasant. It was surprising pleasant, we could easily converse with one another and see where we were going, a real bonus on a rainy day but we couldn't see any other fellow walkers. Today would be a good rest day, especially for my feet and Deborah's knee so, rather than a good walk, a leisurely stroll would be a proper description.

The route needed little interpretation or reference to the map, so there was no need for a frequent stop, another blessing. There was also little to distract us, one farm we came to caused us to stop and observe the sheep, a breed we hadn't seen before; completely black with white socks on. Another farm had a table of fresh fruit and snack bars outside, inviting walkers to take something, and a bowl to receive coins.

We crossed another railway, literally having to walk across the tracks, at which point I unfolded the map to obtain our precise location, obviously this had to be a branch line and not the main Eastern. Disappointed to find we weren't half way there. I was becoming more and more surprised that we hadn't seen anyone else walking today, apart from anyone we already knew. The rain had continued all morning and I was getting more and more wet as the rain began to seep through the outer layers and then the inner ones, even the modern fabric was yielding. We trudged on; the terrain was indeed flat and the scenery not that inspiring, motivated entirely by the wrong reasons, food in the village pub followed by a hot bath.

I could hear civilisation approaching, it had to be the noise of the traffic on the wet A19. Although I couldn't see anything it was ever increasing for the next half an hour and eventually there it was directly across our path, a dramatic contrast to the peace we'd enjoyed for many days, for walkers to traverse at their peril. There we were standing in the rain by the A19 wondering what to do next, a moment where my brain ceased to function accompanied with a glazed expression.

On our left was a lorry driver's café and petrol station, it didn't look a very inviting place but I was certain they would serve a good hot cup of tea so we decided to head over and take a look. Approaching a dated looking shed with steamy windows, suggesting there must be lots of activity inside, being careful not to step into the potholes the size of craters full of oily water, we bravely decided to go in. I wondered whether I'd feel like a fish out of water, I probably looked like one, not wearing oily overalls and carrying the requisite newspaper.

Those thoughts were subdued at the smell of fried food and I was beginning to warm to some real greasy food and a brew, almost forgetting the welcome shelter form the rain. Not being able to see in through the steamy windows we boldly opened the door to enter a very busy lorry driver's haven and joined a small queue giving us time to decide how greasy to go. Fully plated up I turned round to see Robin and Tricia motioning us to join them, at that moment it was good to feel the world was small. There was no need to depart the little café until it stopped raining or conversation dried up so we settled down to dry off, ordering another round of teas each time it felt like we should be leaving.

The rain didn't stop but the time to depart finally came so we all lined up along the A19 waiting for a sufficient gap in the traffic to allow us to sprint across to the North Yorkshire Moors. The village of Ingleby Cross was not much further, it boasted a pub, shop and post office so Deborah suggested we could finally sit, write and send those postcards we'd carried for the last fifty miles. Clearly there was no other option but to head for the pub.

This pub had the perfect vestibule to greet wet and muddy walkers indicating we would be welcome and a blackboard advertising good beer to quench our thirst. I headed straight to the bar and ordered pints for everyone. As I turned round looking for somewhere to sit down I recognised the two ladies, Karen and her sister, we'd seen at breakfast plus the two Australian ladies, Liz and Helen, then the two elderly but fit ladies, Dot and Marg, Chris the plumber and another young chap, occupying half the pub trying to dry out. Naturally we in muzzled in and began to catch up on everyone's news and exchanged experiences. The young chap, also called Chris, was fairly quiet and turned out to be a Canadian cosmologist who worked at the South Pole. His luggage had been lost on the flight over and he didn't yet know where he was staying the next night.

I looked at Deborah acknowledging that the post card writing wasn't going to happen. The unusual thing about this village pub was that the post office and shop were also in the pub, as my eyes scanned the different beers on offer I noticed about four foot at the end of the bar was set aside as the post office counter clearly indicated by the weigh scales and book of stamps, my dad would have smiled.

After we'd shared many amusing walker's tale from all around the world, voices suitably lubricated by a few pints, we felt restored enough to leave the pub behind and set off in search of our B&B wishing to get out of our damp clothes. In a more sombre mood everyone put their waterproofs back on and lined up in the pub vestibule doorway waiting to depart. Staring at the rain each member muttered a soft good bye and, plucking up courage as a fledgling on its maiden flight, stepped outside.

Inspired by the thought of a hot bath, and still smiling about the story of the Australian naked Bush Walker, I thought we had a short journey to our B&B. It wasn't long, however, before I realised how the rain was hampering our progress and making our journey much longer than it ought to be. The cold wet clothes clinging to my skin made movement difficult, after twenty minutes and still no sign of our B&B, I was beginning to get fed up. Finally I indicated to Deborah I was not intending to walk back to the pub for dinner that evening and thankfully she agreed.

As if in disbelief, thinking we'd been walking in an entirely different direction, we ended up back at the A19, clearly identifiable by its Roman straightness and deafening traffic noise. There we stopped and stared at our B&B nestled in a few trees just 10 yards from the roadside. Oh well we'd arrived so we may as well go in. The old house actually looked quite inviting and there was a converted barn which didn't. As we approached we were greeted by three other couples, also walkers, milling around the barn entrance. It was the last thing we wanted to hear a chap in a gruff voice said "there's no one in and the rooms are locked, he won't be back until 5 o'clock". To be fair it was still mid afternoon and the sitting room was open for us to sit in, but this did nothing for our cold wet bodies and the mood could be surmised by the complete lack of conversation which would have been drowned out by the traffic noise anyway.

Have you ever found yourself in a situation where the only conclusion is to do absolutely nothing but wait? This was one of them, like waiting for someone to come out of the operating theatre. Going back to the pub was an option I toyed with for some time but the rain was an obstacle and my tired feet were in favour of staying put. The other thought was; would we be able to sleep above the traffic noise?

I watched the clock as two hours ticked by. Finally I heard a car turn into the driveway so looked up hoping to see, along with everyone else, our host arrive. It was the Sherpa van with our bags, adding insult to injury, a jolly man leapt out singing away to himself as he energetically decanted our bags into the doorway. If he'd asked if we were enjoying our holiday I'm sure someone would have bopped him one.

Another hour passed before our host arrived, quite a young chap who looked like a builder, brandishing a clipboard in a very business like manner with people's names and associated room numbers on it. He made a direct apology to all without any embellishments, for that I was grateful. When he read out our surname name I simply raised my head to make eye contact and reached for our bag, he said room twelve and walked briskly ahead leading us upstairs. He unlocked the door and went in talking about all sorts of things, but it fell on deaf ears. I noticed our room was a loft conversion; everything looked as new as if it had just been built and we were the first to move in. I also noticed the Velux windows in the roof and one window in the gable end giving plenty of light but, we'd lived in a barn conversion, the noise when it rains can be like living inside a drum. I just registered what time breakfast would be served in the morning and he left us to go and deal with the next couple on his list.

Checking out the room we found we were blessed with all mod cons we needed; heated towel rail, kettle, blah blah blah, which significantly helped raise my energy levels. At last, after a day in the rain, the time had arrived to take a hot shower, which had adjustable temperature settings, and put on some dry clothes. I didn't care if they were clean or not, being dry was the most important thing.

Lying on the bed with a cup of tea, looking up at the rain hammering on the windows, I reflected on the journey today and concluded I'd been completely emotionally drained rather then physically drained. I like fresh air, especially in the bedroom, so I had to verify that opening a window would be intolerably noisy and I was right, all the windows would have to stay firmly shut.

After a long period of contemplation discussions began on what we should do for dinner. I'm sure our host listed some options when I wasn't listening and it soon became clear Deborah hadn't taken in what he said either. Preferring not to walk out again in the rain we decided to put out all the food that was in our rucksacks. Thankfully, being in plastic bags, this had kept dry and to my surprise there were several chocolate bars, a packet of peanuts, two oranges and a boiled egg. What more did we need, clearly a starter, main course and pudding was all laid before us.

Decision made, stay in, watch the rain, have an early night.

Chapter 13

I woke a couple of times in the night, probably due to the unusual environment for this journey and mostly the traffic noise, however I instructed my brain to block it out managed to doze off again. Dawn came but there was no sunshine streaming in through the window just a dull light through the drizzle gradually awakening my senses. When it finally came time to get out of bed I felt surprisingly rested so couldn't complain.

Another great day ahead, I cheerfully told myself, stepping into the shower primarily to treat myself to another dowsing of hot water while it was available, already wondering what our next accommodation might be like. For some reason I felt there was an urgency about getting going that day, Clay Bank Top was 13 miles, but I needed to devote time to getting fully ready.

Consulting the Guide book to see what lie ahead the most useful information that I noticed was the presence of a walker's café en route, hmmm I thought, no need for sandwiches. "We'll dine out today my dear at Lord Stones café" I exclaimed. The next important note was about our lodgings and the fact that we'll need to phone for a lift from Clay Bank Top to somewhere called Great Broughton, which for the life of me I couldn't find on the map. When we arrive at Clay Bank top we need to phone Margaret who will send her daughter to collect us. I shared that with Deborah then we descended to the main house for breakfast, making a quick dash across the courtyard in the drizzle.

The front door opened into a large kitchen where the same chap who'd greeted us yesterday was stood in front of a massive four oven AGA.

Everything looked orderly; food on the left, pans on top and plates on the right. There were a surprising number of guests, or should I say all the tables were occupied which made it look busy. Thankfully there were the Australian ladies, Liz and Helen, I didn't recall them saying they were staying here but that was a blessing and they invited us to squeeze in on their table. The chap came over and immediately set out some knives and forks and without thinking about it, completely forgetting my manners, I said two poached eggs on.

We struck up a lively conversation trying to enthuse about the day ahead, while watching the chap prepare breakfast, I hadn't met any of the others before, Liz and Helen had stayed in the main house and chose to dine there last night too. That was all news to Deborah and me. Thankfully no one asked what we did last night.

It looked like the chap was running the whole place on his own, despite his organised approach to cooking he was clearly stretched to breaking point. I couldn't help thinking he needed an assistant, concerned that my breakfast might be cold. We waited for what felt like an age, watching him juggle the pans on the AGA. Thankfully it arrived hot, I ate all there was but, to be honest, I was left still feeling a bit hungry. I was deeply engaged in trying to understand the mind set of Oliver Twist when Deborah voiced we should be getting ready to set off.

Despite the drizzle I was happy get going again, I had no regrets leaving this place and I was now keen to move on. Striding past the pub again we left the village, crossed another main road, and looked up at Arncliffe Woods. Cliff is an appropriate word to describe the ascent we would have make. Our goal was to reach a transmission mast that we could see on top of the hill, a landmark I'd mentally noted last night when preparing for the next day, ha!

The Map, however, indicated a several mile detour to get to this mast so here was our first dilemma of the day; do we climb straight up or take a gradual incline traversing up over several miles? As we left Ingleby Cross we passed a Church which had some tempting cake and an offertory box by it purposely set out for walkers. A generous portion of Ginger Cake provided the additional supplement to breakfast I required whilst we deliberated over which route to take. In the end we opted for the long route, thinking the straight up path would be wet and muddy and consequently more tricky than it looked.

Behind us I recognised Chris, the guy who bought me a pint in Reeth, and his wife whose name escaped me. They weren't quite close enough for normal voice to be heard so he acknowledged me with a single wave of an arm. I thought they must be gaining on us so I prepared to discuss the option of the straight up rout again when I noticed they'd stopped for some cake just as we had. I thought they'd catch us up in a few minutes then, blow me, when I turned round five minutes later they were nowhere to be seen. I began to wonder if they knew a short cut, I even began asking my wife where else they might have gone to satisfy my inquisitive nature.

After a few minutes I started to focus again on our chosen route thinking we often search for a short cut in life to achieve our goals but inevitably they are won by hard work and determination. Encouraged by that truth I put my head down and marched onwards and upwards through the rainy forest happy with our chosen route, encouraged further, after another twenty minutes, when we could see Karen, the policewoman, and her sister sporting a very bright yellow waterproof. After a very brief update on yesterdays travels they announced they were lost. "Not to worry" I said, extracting the map, "we're all heading for the transmitter mast on top of the hill, it can not be possible to miss that landmark" my words becoming slower as I realised we'd gone wrong and turned off to early.

It wasn't at all possible to see any landmarks from the forest floor, we were in a classic case of "can't see the wood for the trees". Being the only bloke I decided we should carry on until we meet the route that goes straight up, which we did until Karen and her sister refused to go any further as there was no obvious route at all and the ground was becoming increasingly infirm. It was true, we were completely off the path but I knew what direction we needed to go in. I explained the merits of persevering, and convinced Deborah that we'd be fine to carry on, Karen and her sister listened politely until I'd finished then turned back. I was surprised the Policewoman wasn't prepared to take a slight risk.

During our climb up the hill, a route that clearly no one had ever done before, I reassured Deborah by saying that the police would naturally choose the safer option, it's a consequence of their training. However as we struggled for grip traversing a very steep boggy hillside there was an argument to support their decision as one slip and it could be several hundred feet before one of us came to rest and, assuming there were no bones broken, you'd be left with the same climb again rather like the proverbial spider in the bath scenario.

More by luck than judgement we arrived exactly where we wanted to be; right by the transmitter mast. Deborah and I looked at one another expressing surprise and relief without saying a word. There was no sign of the two ladies so we carried on following the proper route now which was clearly marked. After a while we joined a well walked route which I later found out was the Cleveland Way. This was more cheerful, open space, no severe gradients and hope for fine weather later as the clouds were starting to break. To add further comfort to our journey the Cleaveland way follows a ridge. I could compare the route on the map and also the white path running along the ridge contrasted against the green grass. It was visible for miles and miles ahead. I could see no one ahead confirming that the two ladies must be behind us. We decided to set a goal and head for the highest point we could see in the distance where we would then take a rest. Happy that a pleasurable day lay ahead of us we strolled on, secretly relieved that we'd managed to get up the hill unscathed, it would no doubt be a topic of discussion later that evening over a pint.

There were many miles ahead of us before Lord Stones Café and lunch but the rain was easing off, or rather it was being blown away by an increasing wind, so we were confident we would be there in time. Compared to the Lakes, today's walk was flat but the occasional climb brought back memories of our earlier days in the Lakes and we chose to rest for a while here and there to recuperate.

There were just a few drops of rain left in the air and we were now able to see a few distant walkers, too far away to identify them but no doubt some we would be acquainted with. I took out my wallet to count the cash, checking we had enough to buy lunch and dinner, having no expectation they could process plastic cards in these remote parts.

We strolled on enjoying the day for what it was. A steep decent to cross a B road reminded me I had other muscles in my legs. At last there was a sign for the café, which simply couldn't be ignored, inviting us in for a welcome rest. To me it looked like something resembling a cave built out of the local stone with plenty of seats outside for muddy people like ourselves. It was busy, no doubt a mandatory stopping place for all walkers, although some customers had made the effort and come by car.

Robin and Tricia were sat outside, no surprise and beckoned us over to join them. It was an opportunity to shed the outer layers and hang them up, employing our walking sticks as best we could, to allow them to dry off a bit. Having no time constraints makes stopping for lunch all the more pleasurable, the menu had a bountiful choice, albeit café food as expected, including locally made Kate and Sydney pie which took my fancy. By the time we'd deliberated over the menu and caught up on the day's trekking with Robin and Tricia we were joined by our Australian friends, Liz and Helen who, having chosen what they wanted, proceeded to enter the café and order for all of us. Due to the long queue and the need for others to take a nature break I found myself alone at the table for a while. Occupied with my own thoughts on how the walk was going I was joined by a hungry chaffinch which plucked up enough courage to hop on my table and eat the remains of an old burger just a few feet away from me. I then noticed a blackbird and robin were closing in, but when Deborah returned and they all retreated, at which point I grabbed the camera assuming they would return and as soon as she'd sat down which they did.

After the others returned and settled down the birds came back, moving the discussion to include the Kukabourough, it was becoming an attractive feeding ground. The next thing we knew there were half a dozen Guinea Fowl marching under all the tables devouring whatever morsels had fallen to the ground, followed by a scruffy peacock. It certainly gave me an opportunity to use the camera in other modes than landscape and the birds were a source of amusement for all the diners. Quite some time had passed before our food finally arrived but we were not disappointed with the quality, it made a welcome change from the usual packed lunch, and the large mug of hot tea.

I could have stayed until the sun went over the yard arm but we still had some miles to walk. We were all staying in B&B's around Broughton but not the same one. Robin made a useful comment that we may not get a phone signal to call ahead for our lifts to our B&Bs that night. I took his comment on board and we set off starting with a steep climb, weighed down by lunch of course, up to Cringle Moor.

It wasn't as bad a Kidsty Pike up the top but it was blowing a whooley and the waterproofs were necessary, not for the rain, but to reduce the wind chill. To mark the occasion we took one another's photographs looking out to Darlington, as we were battered by the wind, but we didn't stay long. Liz and Helen set off at marching pace, I think to escape the wind, and we began to spread out again going at our own pace, those of us fatigued by the days walk straggling behind. As we approached Wainstones, Deborah and I found ourselves alone again. The Wainstones, as the name might suggest, are a rock feature. I could see a group of uncharacteristically dark rocks, rising up that had resisted being weathered by time. I recalled someone over lunch saying they look like something you might decorate the top of a cake with, but clearly on a different scale. Personally I couldn't see it, but then I don't make cakes.

There was an opportunity to do some rock climbing if one so chose but negotiating them was arduous enough. Clay bank top was now within haling distance and with tired legs we slowly descended the steep rocky slope to the road, to find Liz and Helen waiting for their lift, soon to be joined by Robin and Tricia.

I was still rummaging for our B&B details when a car pulled up and Liz and Helen got in, with a quick wave off they went. Robin had already phoned and said their lift would be here in a few minutes. I dialled the number we were given; I was to ask for Margaret's daughter who will come and collect us so that's what I did. I spoke to Margaret alright, she sounded an elderly lady, but the whereabouts of her daughter were unknown to her. She thought her daughter might have taken the children swimming or she might be feeding the chickens. I asked again if we could have a lift and she said she didn't drive, at which point I could sense things were not going to plan. Margaret added people who stay at her B&B usually walk down through the forest into Broughton at which point I gave up and told her that's what we'll do then.

I now had to explain our predicament to my very weary wife which, as you can imagine, was not well received. We were both tired and were expecting a lift and a hot bath, not another 2 mile walk through some forest which, I didn't mention to Deborah, wasn't even on my map!

Crossing the road Deborah saw a footpath signed Broughton and set off in a huff soon leaving me 100s of yards behind as I was going at a pace my tender feet would allow. It wasn't raining anymore but it reminded me of another occasion we went "the extra mile" so I replayed that event to occupy my mind: It was the Saturday after my dad had died and we were in my parent's home sorting through his things when the phone rang. I was still upset after the recent events of a tragic road accident but I answered the phone and a lady asked "have you still got the bed for sale?" At first I hadn't a clue what she was on about, thinking she had a wrong number. Then I remembered my parents wanted to sell a spare bed they had, to free up space in one of the bedrooms. I asked where she had seen the advert and she said it was in the Peak Advertiser. I didn't doubt her and assumed that dad had sent a letter to put the advert in the Newspaper weeks earlier but it had only just been published. Without thinking, perhaps subconsciously realising the bed was no longer required anyway, I said "yes". She said she would come over to look at it within the hour, I nearly said "just wait until we've removed the body" as a joke.

She came over and said she liked it going on to explain at length that she needed it when her son comes to stay with her. I really wasn't listening and got the feeling she lived on her own, but the deal was done. There was something I'd agreed to, however, which I hadn't thought through. She'd asked if I could deliver the bed and I said I'd do it later that day, this lady only lived about 10 miles away. To my surprise we actually found a plastic bag big enough to fit the mattress in and managed to bend it enough to fit it into the boot of my car. I improvised a roof rack and roped this wooden bed on top of the car and Deborah and I set off. We arrived at this ladies house thinking this has actually been a blessing; we were getting rid of a bed we no longer needed and this would help her out at the same time. When we arrived she greeted us at the doorstep and, to my amazement, asked if we could take it upstairs. For some reason I can't explain why I agreed to do that too, but that was our extra mile that day. As we entered her house carrying the bed I could see she lived in a lovely old stone built cottage with a narrow winding staircase and ornaments hung on all the walls. Somehow, with Deborah bringing up the rear, we missed every ornament and managed the wooden frame into her bedroom then looked at one another thinking the mattress is not going to be possible.

Very apprehensive, and now quite weary, we lifted up the mattress and before I'd had time to think about what we were doing it was in the bedroom! I can only say that another force helped manoeuvre the mattress up those stairs, not an ornament was disturbed, it was amazing. Deborah and I looked at one another afterwards asking how did that happen?

Strolling down to Broughton through the forest we needed some of that "extra mile" energy, even thought it was down hill I could tell Deborah's energy reserves had ran out and what she had left was turning into anger.

As we emerged from the forest onto a lane, there was not a soul insight but there was a signpost to Broughton 1 ½ miles. At least we were walking side by side now and were exchanging words although it couldn't be construed as conversation. After twenty minutes a car drove past and we started to come across a dwelling or two then, as if marking our entrance to Broughton itself, a pub. It was closed. The more tired Deborah became, the more annoyed she was, asking where was this B&B? I had an address and a road name but no idea how far it might be and there was no one about to ask. We carried on walking, observing all the street names, and just as we were about to exit Broughton we looked down a street to see old lady standing in the middle of the road frantically waving at us. "That must her" I said.

As we approached Deborah's annoyance boiled over uncharacteristically and she launched into the whys and wherefores of our lift, or more to the point, lack of it, and how this had turned into an absolutely dreadful day. I was taken by surprise at Deborah's attitude and the old lady was clearly taken aback. Just as Deborah finished saying "we never realised we'd have to walk so far from Clay Bank Top" the old lady simply said "you chose to do the walk!" which immediately defused the situation and a level of civility returned.

Margaret led us straight into her house and on into the conservatory where she had laid out a splendid welcome cream tea. She sat us down, poured a most welcome cuppa, and buttered a scone. It had the desired effect and Deborah immediately returned to normal, well almost but not quite, gradually becoming apologetic for her behaviour.

There was one other coaster in our B&B, Chris the Canadian Cosmologist, who we'd met in the pub at Ingleby Cross. He'd arrived on foot, by choice of course, hours ago having meticulously planned his route, deliberately turning off the main route just before the Wainstones to cut through the forest and save several miles. The mention of the Wainstones then turned the conversation to two ladies, who'd stayed at Margaret's last week, and had the misfortune to find a dead walker at the Wainstones earlier that day, either having fallen or having had an heart attack I imagine, but the actual cause of death wasn't known.

Chris had an interesting existence as a Cosmologist at the South Pole where he lived many months of the year. He'd flown over from Canada with his partner to start the walk but their luggage got lost, by the time they were reunited with their luggage they didn't set off from St Bees until 5.00pm that evening so they walked 60 miles in two days to catch up with their planned schedule including the difficult route over Red Pike, High Stile and Haystacks. Not surprisingly this resulted in sever blisters and his partner couldn't carry on so she flew home. He'd reduced the number of miles for a few days to allow the blisters to heal and was now phoning ahead each day to find somewhere to say.

After discussing the big bang theory and how defrosting food at South Pole winter temperatures has to done in three stages, it started to rain. Margaret's thoughts turned to her washing on the line and I felt obliged to dash out and help her bring it in.

Looking at the photos around the house it was obvious she once lived on a farm and her husband had recently died, being such an active lady it seemed running a B&B was a sensible, and suitable, way of living her life to the full and it was certainly keeping her busy. There was no good time to ask this question but I said "could we have a lift back to Clay Bank Top in the morning?" She seemed slightly put out saying she would phone her daughter later, it should be alright but she now charges £2 for petrol. I didn't say it but I would happily pay ten times the price. Chris, of course, said he would have to walk back else his journey on foot would not be continuous. Deborah looked happy.

After the third cup of tea and a similar number of scones filled with home made jam, I decided it was time to freshen up. I took our bags upstairs being careful of all the ornaments hanging up the staircase. The views from our room were fantastic, I don't know what I was looking at they were simply serene and I'd like to think the earlier trauma and our gruelling day on foot was now forgotten.

Following Margaret's recommendation, come 7.00pm, we set of for the pub in search of food. Putting my boots on for ½ mile walk came as a painful shock and the walk to the pub was a very gentle stroll I can tell you.

As we walked through the door into the pub Robin had seen us and was already adding another table to theirs so they could accommodate six of us. They were seated with Karen, the policewoman and her sister, who's name I never did catch. Turning round I saw Chris sat on his own with a pint and a menu, I told him to come and join us but he said he had a cold and didn't want to share it with us, after the second time of asking I allowed him his solitude, explaining to the others the reason he gave for not wanting to join us. Strange he didn't mention his cold earlier.

The food and beer were worth going the extra mile for and the conversation was light hearted, (apart from the two dead walkers we'd now heard about), which rounded off the day on a good note. Everyone was aiming to have an early night.

After all this time someone finally told me the correct pronunciation of the village, it was Brow-ton, and not Brought-on as I'd been pronouncing it. Maybe that's why we had to walk.

Today we'd been tested to the limit. I thought of Shackleton's Antarctic expedition whose family motto was "by endurance we conquer". Our true character had been revealed. It's important to know your limit on the day but more important that your character remains intact.

Chapter 14

The three of us sat in the kitchen with Margaret cooking away proving an unlimited supply of toast, scrambled eggs, tea, accommodating everyone's culinary wishes. She was clearly enjoying being the host.

Today the schedule said fifteen miles but I reckoned we only had about ten to do, as our accommodation was closer, the day after however we would have to do eighteen miles. Our route today would follow many of the old mining railways so, presumably, it was going to be fairly flat across the top of the Yorkshire Moors, once we got our lift up to Clay Bank Top.

I'm pleased to say parting company with Margaret was on the best of terms and I'd recommend her hospitality to anyone. We'd had a very restful night and my feet had recovered sufficiently for the next day. Her daughter duly arrived on time and we bundled into her car and she told us a few tales about the walkers she'd given a lift to. After a short drive we were back at Clay Bank Top and said farewell willingly handing over two pounds to cover her petrol costs.

I presumed Chris was still climbing his way through the forest as neither he nor anyone else was in sight. There was some way to go before we would meet the old dismantled railway and the day started in true to fashion with a hike, just to warm up the limbs, to "Round Hill" the highest summit in Yorkshire". As soon as we started to climb the wind grew stronger blowing and the rain more horizontal, thankfully, on our backs. We stopped to put on all our waterproofs, tightening every cord to help prevent the billowing effect. I was so pleased we weren't walking face on into this weather. As we got nearer the summit the wind continued to increase still further and at the top we were being blown along, our feet hardly touching the ground, thankfully in the direction we wanted to go.

We were now on open heath land with no shelter for miles, it was the first day I hadn't seen sheep, there were just a couple of brightly coloured walkers in the distance, possibly Liz and Helen, and that was it. The dismantled railway soon came into view and we could clearly see our route ahead, getting lost looked impossible for once. I stopped briefly to look at my map to see where we were heading, the aptly named Bloworth Crossing.

I can't imagine what was so important they went to all the trouble to build this railway up here, quite clearly something once was, but I wasn't stopping for a history lesson on a day like this. This place did have a beauty of its own, mile upon mile of heather, some areas burnt to force new growth, some very boggy and some very rocky areas. A bird of prey was gliding at high altitude, just visible against the grey sky, and occasionally I heard a squawk above the noise made by the wind. I hoped the bird of prey wasn't expecting me to come to grief out here.

Our destination was the Lion Inn and our route was, quite simply, to follow this dismantled railway and we would get there. After an hour or so the wind died down, I think this was due mostly to how it was funnelled by the shape of the hills, and the walk was becoming much more pleasurable.

The main event of the morning was passing two walkers coming the other way, seeing them being blown about was quite amusing, then I realised they must have had the same thoughts when looking at us. It was too windy to try and talk so we just smiled, when I looked back they'd taken the fork at Bloworth Crossing heading for the Cleveland Way, rather than St Bees, so I figured they were just out for a day trip which made me wonder what day of the week was it?

I caught a glimpse of a bird in the heather ahead, it was a grouse so I paused, pointed it out to Deborah, and slowly reached for the camera. It was nestled in the heather and hadn't seen us. We watched it for some time, its characteristic motion and behaviour reminding me of a known Whisky advertisement. We were there a good ten minutes watching it and photographing it, a survivor of the glorious 12th as grouse shooting would be popular in this area. Perhaps one will be on the menu tonight.

We agreed to walk one more hour before stopping for a break, at this rate we could be at the Lion Inn for late lunch. As the old railway track meandered around the hills we could see two brightly yellow coloured walkers ahead again and, such was the changing scenery, began to speculate who they were. There were also a couple a mile or so behind us and suddenly I was planning where and how long to stop for our break for fear of being overtaken, or having to make conversation, what a selfish thought, then perhaps I was enjoying the solitude of this place so much I wanted it to myself.

Eventually we stopped and perched on a couple of wooden posts, which once looked to be part of a gate a century ago, it was the only structure left standing for miles around. With just a few days left on our journey it was a poignant moment so I paused to reflect on our experience so far while we took on water and a biscuit. Another hour and a building became discernable on the horizon, silhouetted on the skyline, miles away which I took to be the Lion Inn, we still had some walking to do.

As we came round the next hillside the two walkers in bright clothing came back into view and before long we could see it was Liz and Helen. I presumed we caught them up because they'd taken a break and so we walked together and began conversing. As it turned out I was almost right, they informed me they'd actually stopped for a nature break, too much information leaving me wondering if the wind had blown it far. One that note it was clear there would be room for a late lunch and we were all headed to the Lion Inn which was now in full view. For the first time I was also told they were headed for the same B&B.

Having stopped and dawdled about Robin and Tricia were now hot on our heels, no doubt with renewed enthusiasm at the sight of the Lion Inn, and our trek along the dismantled railway had come to an end. For me it was a welcome relief from hours of battering by the wind and rain. I took a brief and probably last look back along the route, which I could only just make out as the mist was descending, before striding into the Lion Inn stopping to take my wet boots off and park my walking stick in the entrance lobby.

This was a busy Inn, not surprising as this was the only watering hole for many miles around, also providing accommodation for the many passing walkers. Should you ever feel the need to venture out here, you'll no doubt end up at the Lion Inn, a tempting place to come even if you are not on foot. Unfortunately we didn't have accommodation here but we were going to phone for a lift to our B&B with Liz and Helen, after a pint and something to eat of course. We managed to find a table and squeeze in allowing room for Robin and Tricia, who would no doubt be joining us soon enough. A friendly welcome and efficient distribution of menus from the many staff made me feel at home. To top it off they had Old Peculiar on draft, which for me is a very tempting pint but would have probably finished me off right at that moment, but I know where to come next time. The home made pies were too tempting to resist and, as our walking was basically over for the day, we all nestled down for the afternoon to enjoy one another's tales. I say "enjoy" but the first story was about a chap who died here in the pub yesterday, a fellow walker to boot, he said he wasn't feeling well, went to bed and never woke up. So we drank to the one who was blown off Striding Edge, the one found dead at Wainstones, and the one found dead here. It could have easily turned into one of those times when the beer becomes fuel for a deep eschatological discussion until the world slipped out of focus.

The time came to make the call for a lift to our B&B which, this time, arrived within five minutes. Deborah Liz Helen and I collected our things, chucked them into the boot, waved a fond farewell to Robin and Tricia and climbed into a 4x4 to be driven to a B&B in Rosedale by our host. He was a talkative chap who unfortunately thought he was also amusing. Some information I found useful but, possibly due to having a few to many pints, I was struggling to look interested. In fact I was so conscious of the stale cigarette smoke in the vehicle I was trying not to feel ill.

The girls, however, seemed to be interested and we did get a factual account on how the heather has to be burnt regularly to manage the moorland so the grouse can feed on new shoots plus some riveting other stuff before we pulled up at an old three story stone terraced dwelling miles from anywhere. We were so far from anywhere else he insisted on driving us to the pub that evening for dinner and collecting us again. There was obviously some arrangement he had with the local landlord, hoping my appetite would recover, we all accepted the offer. All out for dinner at 7.00pm.

We jumped out the car and I grabbed as many bags as I could then I saw him looking at my boots as if to say you're not coming in here with those on. We all took our boots off and I was beginning to wonder if this was a B&B that welcomed walkers. His wife greeted us and held the door open so I wouldn't scratch it with all the bags I was carrying and then pointed to the visitor's book which we had to sign before he handed out our room keys. I stopped to think when Liz and Helen were also given a key to a double room and I was left concluding that it wasn't to save cost.

Ascending to our room I couldn't help think of the pub in Patterdale, which had the narrow staircase and deep ruts on the walls at each bend, cut by the corners of suitcases as occupants had tried to negotiate their way up and down. Our room turned out to be half way up to the attic, with similar narrow stairs, and as I wound my way up wielding our bag I became slightly more attentive to the task, especially since the owner was following me. Perhaps it was the way he saw me falling out the pub earlier that caused him concern, not to worry as I negotiated the stairs perfectly not leaving the slightest of visible scratches.

Our room was a bit small, actually it was unbelievably tiny with three of us crammed in, and he started to explain something about the hot water system which fell on deaf ears. As far as I was concerned the room had the necessary paraphernalia which were about to fully utilise, having plenty of time to perform a full laundry before dinner, take a shower and get changed. As there were just two more days left on this journey, it was an opportunity not to be missed; once all the hard work was done it was immediately followed by a well earned lie down.

Just before 7.00pm, suitably dressed for an outing to the local, we descended the tight staircase and waited in the TV lounge for the ladies and our host the driver. I sat there scanning the multitude of ornaments, each of which must have been purchased to remind them where they'd been and no doubt told their family story. I had come to the conclusion years earlier all this stuff can clutter up your life, the objects become more precious than the memories and you can become a slave to them. I found the best cause of action is to de-clutter life and have a thorough purge of all the material things that we unwarily accumulate over time and have become a burden; moving house provides an ideal opportunity for such a cleansing.

The ladies arrived looking all dressed up and sat for a chat. Probably the first time the four of us had the opportunity to share our lives stories more intimately but we'd only just started when our driver came in and asked if we were ready. Not wishing to disrupt his schedule, the smell on his breath indicating he'd just finished a fag, we jumped to our feet and enthusiastically climbed back into the 4x4 asking where we were going, not that I really cared as I had no idea where we were.

As we drove off he started his amusing banter, perhaps he was a coach driver in his former life, but to be honest I wasn't taking any of it in and I've still no idea where he drove me. As we said au revoir he said just tell the chap at the bar to give me a call when you're ready, I left Deborah to note his phone number and what B&B we were staying in just in case.

The old pub was a typical village local, able to cater for all generations, and the four of us found a quite corner and asked for a menu. Conversation resumed where we left off earlier, as if we'd known each other for ages. Relative to Deborah and I they were fit active youngsters and were apt to do some bush walking, whatever that was, and we were invited to join them when we visit Australia.

Helen's dad was once an Engine Driver, in the days of steam trains, and on one occasion had met the Queen. Anyhow one of the places we would be walking through on our journey had a working steam railway so they had planned to spend a day there on the steam trains, as part of their holiday, in remembrance of her dad. Conversation was brought to an abrupt halt when Helen said she had just found out that the day they had planned to do this was now advertised as a special Diesel Day! Thankfully comfort for her came as a lady walked in with a Toy Poodle dog. Helen had one herself so she went to stroke it and chat to the owner. That's good, a "Poodle fix" said Liz.

As the evening progressed "Diesel Day" became a wry remark and the ever bountiful supply of good food and beer, which I'd enjoyed nearly every day on this journey, ended our day on a cheerful if somewhat reflective note. I'd even found room for a pudding which was most unusual and must have put me in a strange mood as I offered to pay the bill, the Australians put up some resistance but Deborah fought them off. The generous gesture was appreciated by all the ladies and before I'd signed the cheque they'd made the call and our driver was outside, within a few more minutes I was sound asleep.

Chapter 15

I woke early, my mind still contemplating our journey to date, so I laid there in bed looking at the clouds. There was no noise, no smell, nothing to distract my senses I waited for a toilet to flush or the smell of bacon to arouse my senses but nothing. Two days more on our journey, as man and wife we would have many memories to share later. Deborah had been a great support as always, how she puts up with me I'll never know. She'd probably say "it works both ways". The weather looked fine again so I couldn't see why we shouldn't make today's destination; Egton Bridge a mere twelve miles, our penultimate day.

To start from where we left off meant a drive back to the Lion Inn, that's where we had to leave our bags for collection, so there was a strict departure time today of 8.30am. After reconciling myself to all that, I mustered the energy to get up. I took a long shower and got ready in my own little world, in a very methodical manner, paying particular attention to plasters, socks and comfort. Twelve miles didn't sound that far and I was expecting a sensation of going down hill for a change, a gradual decent perhaps as we approach the coast. Deborah was ready, I was ready, so we descended gracefully for breakfast where a table for the 4 of us was laid out. Yet again we were the first to arrive so we helped ourselves to some fruit juice and waited patiently and quietly looking out of the window onto the back garden. I was in one of my thoughtful moods I suppose, staring out of the window and not really wanting to engage with anyone else, but I decided to make an effort and, against the odds, struggle through with deep resolve and enthusiasm.

Soon enough Liz and Helen joined us, they were in a buoyant mood and ready for the day ahead. We were not alone as I thought, the host arrived to take our order and said another walker arrived last night having done twenty five miles and had suffered the consequences; he had very swollen toes and could hardly walk. Before long he came into the dining room, said hello and then sat on a table of his own. He looked an elderly chap, probably still in work, and I felt it right to say something. In a brief conversation it turned out he had actually walked twenty five miles yesterday and he said the only walking he'd done before this Coast to Coast was around where he lived in the city of Birmingham. Despite his lack of preparation he made it quite clear that he was determined to finish what he'd started. I was struggling to find a suitable response, deliberating whether to say an encouraging "well done, very courageous" or "you wassock". He seemed the independent type and was happy with our brief conversation. He never mentioned a partner and nothing more was said, I had to admire his courage and tenacity.

Breakfast was punctuated with more whitty comments from our host, some smiled at his wry humour to keep the mood light hearted, I did contribute and say the food was very palatable.

The time came to depart and I was waiting eagerly outside the kitchen door for our packed lunches, the door wasn't quite closed and through the gap I could see his wife shuffling her pans over a massive AGA. I waited long enough for Deborah to arrive and lined up our boots ready for stepping into then the two ladies arrived, conveniently at exactly the same time as the kitchen door opened, to be greeted with the readily prepared food parcels. Our host had opened the visitor's book and was holding out a pen, inviting us to comment, which Deborah took. It was judgemental of me but, thinking he just wanted some testimonials to increase his tourist board star rating, I decided to busy myself by packing my rucksack, hastily putting on my boots to make a beeline for the 4x4 in the hope I wouldn't be asked to comment.

As we drove off I was told the walker with swollen toes had already set off on foot, so I kept silent pondering his raison d'être, and then my own. One final verbal quip, finger pointing from our host as we drove by, related to "Fat Betty" a white stone statue resembling something vaguely fat and female at which a passing walker should leave a gift of food and take something that has already been left. At this remark Helen remembered a chewy bar that has accompanied her all the way from Melbourne and decided she had finally found a purpose for it.

I said a pleasant farewell as we alighted at the Lion Inn, after all we'd been well looked after. Having never before arrived at a pub so early in the day I wondered what the collective noun for a group of walkers might be as I stared at the many gathered in the car park. An "Amble" might be the usual term but today "Galoshes" seemed more appropriate, at least that was the picture I had looking at the dozens assembled outside the Lion Inn. I looked up at the dark clouds being blown over and asked Deborah, in my usual ignorance, "is today going to be muddy"? Robin, Tricia, Karen the policewoman, and her sister were among the crowd as well as many other familiar faces we'd become acquainted with over the last week or so. Not being a fan of crowds I managed to rouse an encouraging "hello", plus an expression that I felt indicated what we'd accomplished, so far.

The fine weather I witnessed earlier had soon been displaced by low cloud blown over by a stiff breeze and I couldn't decide what to wear, Galoshes I had not. By the time I'd faffed about getting my bootlaces tightened and my jacket sorted nearly all the other Galoshes were well under way marching back up the road towards Fat Betty. I found myself several hundred yards behind, but not far enough behind to comfortably take a pee without being seen in the open moor land. I began to wonder, having just left the pub, if it was psychosomatic. Finally I saw a ditch which looked dry and deep enough to conceal me so I took the risk and went in, much to my relief. I was particularly wary when stepping into it as once upon a time I ended in one up to my neck in foul water.

As with many other activities walking is one I wouldn't recommend on a full bladder so, having dealt with the call of nature, I was able to press on and within ten minutes had joined the others just before they arrived at Fat Betty. I reached for the camera to capture the moment Helen Liz and Deborah celebrated another landmark on their journey leaving a snack for those who would happily come after us. They all seemed very pleased with this act of giving and taking, perhaps that's something we don't do enough of. We should give to others, not expecting to receive, that's not difficult but how often do we do that? We should also receive with gratitude, which can be more difficult. I wonder how Fat Betty came to be in existence. As

I looked all around, as far as I could see, I thought this must be today's summit and therefore it's all down hill from here.

There was quite a stretch of road left to walk and I was looking forward to leaving it behind. Looking back I see a group of other walkers which helped, psychologically at least, to push me onward. I was happily pondering to myself and we'd walked another mile or so before Deborah eventually broke my silence and, to my surprise, showed me what she'd taken from Fat Betty; an Australian Chocolate bar, something we could savour later no doubt.

I found the open moorland was becoming a drag, my feet were not enjoying walking on tarmac today, which reminded me of the section of road to Danby Whiske, and I could see many walkers strung out along the route negating the necessity to look at the map. Deborah had also begun to look uncomfortable, eventually indicating she wanted a pee and looking at me as if somehow I should know where there would be a suitable place. I spent the next quarter mile looking at the miles of open landscape that surrounded us for a crater for her to squat in. It was another mile before I pointed decisively at a shallow dip insisting she would be fine over there, no one would see, but mind any nettles.

Music: Albinoni Oboe concerto in D minor

I became more heartened when I could see and feel we were actually beginning to descend, even catching the occasional glimpse of the sea through the mist, which the sun was now thankfully starting to burn off. I was contemplating the events along our journey, perhaps I felt some sadness that our journey's end was near, this was, after all, the penultimate day. Although the route was well marked, curiosity got the better of me and I took time out to look at the map wanting to know exactly where we were, to which the answer was Glaisdale More and Glaisdale itself would be the next village.

I'd never been to Glaisdale but the map indicated it had a pub, post office, and a railway station, so in the scheme of things this was a Metropolis. The road had turned into a rocky track leading onward and downward demanding concentration where to tread so conversation, despite the many people near by and within earshot, had dried up. The rocky track led to a promontory providing an excellent viewing point across to Glaisdale so we took the opportunity to stop.

I didn't find walking today particularly arduous, I certainly couldn't describe it as exhilarating, which I might use describe Striding Edge for example, but it would be easy to sprain an ankle on the rocky track if you'd ventured out in slippers. No, to be honest, today was a bit of an amble becoming more and more pleasurable as the temperature rose, the sun began to break through the cloud, and as the views became more beautiful my thoughts of the journeys end being sad ones began to turn to positive ones.

The time came for a rest and something to eat, my pondering mood was over, and I'd decided to be sociable so we sat in a cluster with Liz, Helen, Robin, Tricia, Karen her sister, and another couple who were, well, just there. It wasn't until I sat down that I started to absorb the view. It was a view that was worth all the effort, the tired limbs, the sore feet, the weather, the . . . . and having got there I felt rewarded in so many ways. It was a place where I wanted to stay, my senses had switched off from what was going on around me and I couldn't think of any reason to leave, even though in reality there was quite some walking ahead of us and the journey was far from over, a place to remain as long as it took to reflect on what had been achieved.

I looked down over a beautiful place that words can not describe; after all if we could express it with words we wouldn't need music. I was eventually distracted by the sound of a distance aeroplane that was approaching, it had an unusual droning sound that echoed around the valley, I thought it would have been music to some ears at the time of the Second World War, it was a Hurricane I think.

My senses started to respond to someone speaking, I picked up what was being said half way though the conversation. Karen was being the talkative one, flowing with jovial banter in a voice, although not loud, that had attributes which could be heard by all. I caught the part where she mentioned they all saw Deborah having a pee. I said nothing in response but wondered how long it would be until the subject was mentioned again.

Food eventually came to mind so I searched for today's packed lunch offering not expecting great things so as not to be disappointed but it was fine, I take back all I said earlier. Deborah looked happy, no knee problems, my feet were not grumbling, therefore neither was I, so we left our small group and set off to be on our own along the long lane to Glaisdale.

We still had the glorious view to our right and could see Glaisdale in the distance with a glimpse, now and then, of Glaisdale Beck on our right. I was reminded of a walk we've done which includes a track simply named "long lane" to which my feet bore testimony to at the end of that day, so with that in mind I deliberately set a modest pace. Conversation, sparse as it normally was, became punctuated every fifteen minutes by the return of the Hurricane which kept repeating its circuit until we came directly under its flight path. Another topic for conversation and a complete technological contrast to the jet that kept us company on our stage to Orton, if in purpose no contrast at all.

Another watering stop and a couple of hours later Glaisdale arrived as if by surprise. A sleepy village, Yorkshire stone built houses of course, with lanes of such gradient I thought we'd need ropes. Despite the steep decent I managed to come to an abrupt halt outside a butcher's window as my eyes focused on a home made pork pie. Deborah grinned at me and without saying a word opened the door and went in.

When Deborah came out I immediately put my nose in the bag, satisfied with what it told me, all we needed now was somewhere to sit and eat it. We strolled on turning the next corner to find Robin and Tricia sat on a bench munching something very similar to what we had in our bag. There was subdued laughter, as if admitting a degree of envy, but more importantly the mutual appreciation of a fine local pie. They were headed to a B&B in Grosmont for the night so we said our good byes and, if not before, we'd see them in the bar at Robin Hoods Bay.

After a few hundred yards we'd walked from one end of the village to the other passing the pub without hesitation and then the village petrol pump to reach the railway station. A quick read of the timetable indicated trains were known on occasion to stop here. I took the trouble to explain to Deborah this was the line to Whitby, stopping at Grosmont and the North Yorkshire Moors Railway, where Liz and Helen had planned a day on the steam train, the day that had unfortunately for them turned out to be Diesel day.

I turned the page on the map to see a large blue area on the right, the sea, realising we were on the last page. We were at Beggars Bridge, built in 1619, and it seemed appropriate to take some time to rest and read about its history before crossing it. The tree lined river brought a welcome cool air scented with the damp fragrance of woodland flora. There were two routes to Egton Bridge and we'd chosen to take the lesser used one, the one marked with little red dots rather than the big red dashes, which took us up a steep climb to a lane, sadly, leaving the woodland behind. I still couldn't see anywhere pleasant enough to sit and enjoy the pie so, preferring to do it justice, I felt it was best left for supper.

Broom House was our destination for tonight's stay, our legs were now tired, just a few fields to cross to meet a lane going uphill and it should be a few hundred yards on our right. A mile further on and I stopped at the brow of a hill, disappointed to see nothing but fields. I dared to suggest we may have made a mistake so back down the hill we went, passing the footpath that led us to the road in the first place and low and behold there was Broom House. It all became clear, we'd strayed slightly from the footpath on the map so when we met the road we'd already passed Broom House, thankfully we were able to put it down to tiredness and were grateful it hadn't let to a detour of many miles.

Our bags were there to greet us along with a pleasant mannered owner. "Your room isn't quite ready yet would you like to take tea on the lawn"? He said quite seriously. Blimey! I thought, this is a bit posh, and as he led us out to be seated in the garden I could see it was. I almost felt out of place in my sweaty walking gear, splashes of mud all over and no doubt some on my face but we rose to the occasion quickly adopting the mindset and demeanour of the landed gentry. Just as my socks were starting to dry out, as I waved my feet in the gentle breeze, our brew arrived dressed in the finest Royal Doulton, I happened to know that because I worked in an Antique Shop on Saturdays as a boy. It was presented by a waitress dressed as one would expect including the fine white lace. It included scones, cream, jam, butter and other tasty things. "Well, my dear, what a pleasant afternoon after all that stomping about" I exclaimed.

After a while I heard a distant clock chime 5 o'clock, thinking our room must be ready by now we prised ourselves up and went back to reception to find the owner and enquire. I grabbed our bags for fear of paying porterage and followed a lady politely summoned by the owner. This was a lovely Georgian house with some modern, but tasteful, additions like the restaurant and our room, which the lady summoned by the owner led us to. As soon as she left I collapsed onto the bed to relax before trying the shower. Although there was only one day left on our journey it was still necessary to perform the laundry duties.

I was just about to start getting undressed and send my pants and socks for a good scrubbing when there was a knock on the door. The lady returned wittering on apologetically that she would like us to move to another room. No thanks I thought I was quite happy with this one. She persisted and explained they were going to put an American group in the whole of the upstairs and we would be upgraded to a suit on the first floor. At this suggestion we responded by picking up our things and following her again. The room was indeed one of the best I've stayed in, apart from a suit in a hotel in Rome, again an upgrade which I didn't have to pay for, and it had a massive bath big enough to practice the breaststroke. The heated towel rail looked like a genuine Georgian bit of cast iron.

A bath was indeed in order and worth waiting for it filling. Clean and refreshed I left the steamy bathroom robed in white and, rather than adopt my usual lazy approach of flinging myself on the bed, chose to sit in a chair with guilt arms and Queen Anne legs to enjoy the view out of the window. I picked up the conveniently placed menu, noticing they had my favourite beer on draught, so I read it out to Deborah in a voice loud enough to penetrate the bathroom door. It had all we wanted so I suggested we dine here this evening to which she happily agreed. Well it did seem pointless to me looking for anywhere else.

Dining could wait until we'd taken an early evening stroll around Egton Bridge itself, after all we hadn't actually been there yet and the map said there was a pub and railway station. We walked along the river bank flanked by a row of old houses that looked very desirable to live in, the sort of place I could retire to. We came across an old chap fly fishing which echoed the tranquil tone of the place. We found the railway station, denoting one end of the village, but failed to find the pub so, assuming that must be on the other side of the river, turned around and headed back to continue the search.

Completely by chance, although being naturally inquisitive, we noticed some stepping stones which looked like an ancient footpath across the river behind someone's back garden. Feeling brave, the stones just showing their heads above the fast flowing river, we stepped our way across to arrive at the back entrance to the pub. I wondered how many drinkers had come to grief over the centuries crossing the river after a few pints. As it turned out the pub was still closed so we made our way back to Broom House.

As we arrived it occurred to me that we hadn't actually booked a table for diner, thankfully my fears were soon allayed by our accommodating host who also came up with the fantastic suggestion that we have a drink in the lounge whilst we wait. I sat in opulent luxury in the grand Georgian lounge waiting for my favourite pint to be brought to me whilst Deborah read. After my second pint another gentleman came in and sat down, this necessitated breaking the silence. Thankfully it turned out we shared the same goal and having something in common to talk about made for some buoyant conversation. We headed into the dining room with spirits uplifted and eager to attack the final day.

In contrast to tea, in the garden earlier, the restaurant was very modern, even the wood burning stove was modern but clearly some thought had gone into blending the new and old decor. The service and food were excellent and it was probably the best dining experience we'd had on our journey, not forgetting each of the other memorable experiences that all serve to contribute to the whole. I vaguely remember climbing into the enormous bed in our suit and there my day ended.

The romantic Beggars Bridge in Glaisdale

Chapter 16

I n the early hours I woke in agony with a sharp pain in my right foot, the pain woke Deborah too. "Ow my foot" I kept groaning through clenched teeth, until Deborah finally put the light on. I stared at a big red swollen toe in disbelief and began to wonder what had caused it then thought what I really need is a solution and fast. I swung my legs out of bed and tried to stand up but found I couldn't put all my weight on it, I then tried to walk around the bedroom hoping it would ease off.

After ten minutes or more hobbling about in agony I realised walking probably caused it in the first place and I'd just made it worse, perhaps it needed rest, so I laid on the bed again and groaned wondering what I'd done to cause it. Had I twisted my foot when climbing the steep hill after Beggars Bridge? Perhaps I had. Was it jumping on the stepping stones? Could be, I was wearing my trainers last night, was that it? Was it Gout? I'd discussed it with Deborah then she realised what this meant; I might not be walking any more.

She took a look at it and suggested some Ibuprofen to reduce the swelling and some painkillers. I could only agree so she went and found them, well I wouldn't have a clue where they were, I took the maximum dose and lay in bed still pondering my predicament. "You might have to walk the last leg on your own" I said.

The hours ticked by, daylight broke, and I was still awake. The pain killers had certainly helped me rest but would I be able to walk eighteen miles today was the question? Although it was very early I decided to run a hot bath to see if soaking would help so I stood up and concluded that the pills had helped, I least it didn't hurt as much, and since four hours had passed I could take some more so I did.

I concluded that the way forwards demanded a positive attitude, thanking God we'd got this far, that my foot would be healed and there would be hot water out of the bath tap which there was. I must have floated about for an hour before I could hear Deborah stir and put the kettle on. Perhaps she would bring me a cup of tea I thought.

Now convinced there was nothing else I could do I got out of the bath, stared angrily at my foot which was now the same colour as my whole body, and slowly began to walk about getting ready for the day ahead. "How is it?" asked Deborah, I said nothing, responding simply by raising my right foot and facial expression, so she carried on preparing herself for the day ahead. "I've come this far," I said.

I put many pairs of socks on to cushion my feet and staggered into the dining room thinking people will assume I've got a massive hangover. Breakfast arrived swiftly and was spot on, fruit, cereals, eggs on toast, perfect ingredients for a day's walking. By 8.00 o'clock we were ready, the weather looked warm enough so I changed into my shorts, partly that and partly because I felt it was time to behave and look like a real walker. The time came to put my boots on, this was the part that took ages, I took myself into the garden and had to all the laces before I could squeeze my right foot into the boot without screaming. Once the boots were on I jumped up and told Deborah in a determined voice "we're off"!

Looking at one another with some fondness for this place, we couldn't depart Egton Bridge without going over the stepping stones once more, so we agreed a little detour was in order. By the time I got to the stepping stones my right foot felt like it was loosening up but I held back announcing everything was fine, this time treading carefully across the stepping stones rather than doing the circus act I performed yesterday.

After passing the railway station we joined a lane which looked like it was taking us through a country estate. I was grateful it was flat which was one good thing, and surprised to see more than a few walkers already marching towards Grosmont, just a couple of miles away, and even more surprised that we started to pass them.

Grosmont was where most of those we'd met along our journey had stayed last night but, by the time we arrive, I assume they'd be well on their way. For once I was complete wrong, I'd forgotten we'd made quite an early start and the first person we bumped into staring through the window of an art gallery was Caroline. She was nursing her sprained ankle and having a restful day in Grosmont. David was still walking, he'd tagged onto some other walkers and she was going by bus, they were doing what they could to get to the finish. After packing as much information as possible into a few minutes conversation we agreed to meet in the bar later that day, we may even meet David on route, he'd already set off and should be just ahead.

Less than a hundred yards down the road there was Liz and Helen by the level crossing. They we're not difficult to identify wearing their brightly coloured walking gear, no doubt trying to mix in with the train spotting fraternity on their special Diesel Day. Although we hadn't spent much time together it was a joyful greeting and we stopped for a while to talk. I imparted what little knowledge I had of the railway then we bid them a final fond farewell, they would not be walking the last leg until tomorrow and by the time they arrive we'd be long gone.

The route from Grosmont is by road, up a steep hill, for miles. I couldn't see anyone in front or behind us, it was just the wife and I verses the hill. Having felt cold all morning I was now glad I'd put shorts on. A couple of weeks ago I'd have been puffing like a steam train and stopping occasionally to admire the view but today, after two weeks of preparation you might say, I was really enjoying the climb pushing on as much as my body would allow. If asked I'd say we marched relentlessly for three miles up that hill including, in my book, some steep gradients.

Arriving at Sleights Moor I realised this was the highest summit of today, able to see some coastal landmarks and the sea beyond. I was surprised how much our ability had increased over the last two weeks, consequently leading to a realisation of our capability; this walk had become truly satisfying. Everyone will tell you that if you want to succeed it takes practice, perseverance, determination and all that goes with it, well this was one of those rare occasions where I was able to experience the results myself. Approaching the summit I felt like someone crossing the finishing line for a gold medal at the Olympics. I was well satisfied with my modest achievement, feeling invigorated and wanting more, especially having overcoming my painful swollen foot to which I could have easily given into and no one else in the world knows. It just feels good.

Without stopping I continued to stroll on at a lesser pace and after most of the colour had drained from our faces communication resumed sharing our amazement at how effortlessly we'd climbed that last hill. It wasn't long before the cooler wind, coming straight from the sea and blowing across the open moor, made us pick up the pace again in favour of stopping to put more clothes on. For this reason I was grateful for the decent towards Littlebeck and finally some shelter from the valley.

Littlebeck was one of the prettiest if tiniest hamlets I've visited, the beck running right through it as its name suggests. Albeit a brief pause on our journey, as the mood was very much developing into one of progression and conclusion. Moving on we entered dense woodland and followed the beck uphill. It wasn't long before I could hear voices and soon there were three walkers plodding along almost at rest taking photos, blimey one of them was David, as in David and Caroline, who'd sprained her ankle and we'd left in Grosmont that morning, from Australia.

Finally, although I still wanted to march on, I had an excuse to take a breather and catch up on what we'd all experienced. I hadn't seen David for days and I was genuinely please to learn he and Caroline had decided he should carry on walking, fortunately for him he'd latched onto another couple to share his journey with and encourage him. It did seem to me that they were happy to saunter so we bid farewell, until the bar that evening.

The accent through Scary Wood wasn't, however the beck on our right delighted with some spectacular waterfalls, one called Falling Foss, whose beauty tempted one to the edge for a closer look. As if by no surprise we also found Robin and Tricia taking a photo, just by the Hermitage. Robin, one of those chaps with a mind of information enlightened me: It's a huge rock hollowed out in 1790 to create a dwelling so, enthusiastically, we stepped in. He was right; even I could deduce that was a fair amount of chiselling.

To be fair it was lunch time and by now we'd covered half the distance. Robin had heard that what was once a derelict old shack, in the middle of a wood, had become a cafe. His suggestion that we sit down have a cup of tea was welcome. Actually it was called Midge Hall, once a Keepers cottage then a museum and now a café. It was a pretty spot but as we approached I was surprised to find it so busy, we had trouble finding a vacant seat.

Tricia seemed to have the knack of muscling in and obtained a seat for us all. We sat comfortably outside for a good 30 minutes watching people coming and going. Most of them looked to me like day trippers, Robin could see I was puzzled and then told me the car park was less than a half mile away which explained everything.

Although we all set off together it wasn't long before Robin wanted to take another photo and we took the opportunity to march ahead soon to come to the car park and expecting to see an ice cream van. My feet were now a bit weary but thankfully there was just a short climb up a lane and I could see open moor land again. I began to imagine I could smell the sea in the hope this would draw me along like someone cooking bacon on a campsite first thing in the morning.

Unfortunately these happy thoughts had distracted me from looking where we were going and I suddenly found we were in the middle of a peat bog and beginning to sink. Looking back I could see a young couple, who had obviously followed us, mistakenly thinking we knew where we were going. They realised and turned back, heading up hill for dryer ground. Discretion not being the better part of valour I continued in order to show them I knew exactly where I was going, striding across reed beds in order to demonstrate that running through deep water, if you do it fast enough, means you don't actually get your feet wet.

Deborah, sensibly, witnessed my performance then decided to make for higher ground. When we finally reconvened she looked her muddy husband up and down with an expression of disbelief. Nothing was said and we followed in the wake of the young couple who were now ahead of us.

Arriving at a road sign indicating three and a half miles to Robin Hoods Bay we sat down on the grass bank to rest. Several people passed us by and everyone exchanged a few words. After I felt the wind had dried the mud on my face I struggled to my feet, held my hand out to Deborah to haul her up, and we got under way.

After crossing the A171 at Hawkser we were less than a mile from the sea, but not before passing through the ubiquitous caravan park did we come to the coast. At the coast we were greeted by a strong easterly wind, and the sound of ferocious waves that crashed into the cliffs, waves of a magnitude I hadn't previously witnessed. Everything that was behind us was out of sight and out of mind, so too were any related emotions.

I stopped in awe watching the forces of nature at work. I could see Nature could be used, by drawing on parallels, to explain so many things I've often struggled to even begin to comprehend. The visible waves are dark and silent, their journey started many miles out, they finally crash into the rocks in a burst of white foam and what we see dies. At that moment, however, they are reborn into new life and their journey continues as sound. The sound wave now carries on for miles and miles. I could still hear them and you could too if you had sensitive enough ears. Our life's journey is like this.

The crashing waves were keeping us company as we hugged the cliff tops for the last few miles to the Bay, I'd like to think of it as Nature's applause. For the first time today I could clearly see the route a mile or more in front, as well as behind, and realised we were certainly not alone, and worse, the bar would be packed.

Waves of the North Sea

Over our journey we'd met many companions as we ebbed and flowed but now we were all converging as we reached the goal. Accompanied by several other walkers I'd not seen before we started to funnel into Robin Hoods Bay, arriving as if via the back stage door, passing back gardens, through alleyways and side streets, to finally emerge onto the main street, the "stage", to be greeted like heroes. Hero's we were not.

Music: Handel The Arrival of the Queen of Sheba

I clapped eyes on a huge "Well done" sign, written in bold letters on a sheet, held out by Deborah's Mum and Dad, along with many other families who'd come to greet loved ones. After the photo session we continued down the steep hill to the shore to perform the final act of throwing our stones into the sea, we'd done it, Alleluia.

All that remained was to sign the book, whilst ordering a pint, and take a seat outside the bar to greet all those we'd met and congratulate them. Robin and Tricia were not far behind, Caroline was waiting for David and Chris the plumber was with his wife. Chris, who bought me a pint in Reeth, and his wife were already at the bar, Paul and Carly made an appearance along with dozens we didn't personally know but whose faces were familiar.

Chris had thought to check the book to establish that Barbara and Peter had signed it and I was pleased for them. After a couple of hours the euphoria started to die down and we began to say our farewells. As we climbed up the steep hill to start a new journey I wondered when I'll see them again.

I often wonder what happens to a thought, an image or picture that you create in your mind. The food you eat provides the energy and you use the energy to create the thought but where does it go when you've finished with it? Perhaps it's exactly like the waves of the sea I heard earlier and the energy continues on. What if someone, He, was listening to your thought? What if you had ears that could hear what He was saying?

Luke Chapter 8 Verse 8 He that hath ears to hear, let him hear.

The journey home.

Music:
Pietro Mascagni Intermezzo from Cavalleria Rusticana

Throwing the Pebble at Robin Hoods Bay